HOW TO DRAW GRAFFITI

SOPHIA PRESS

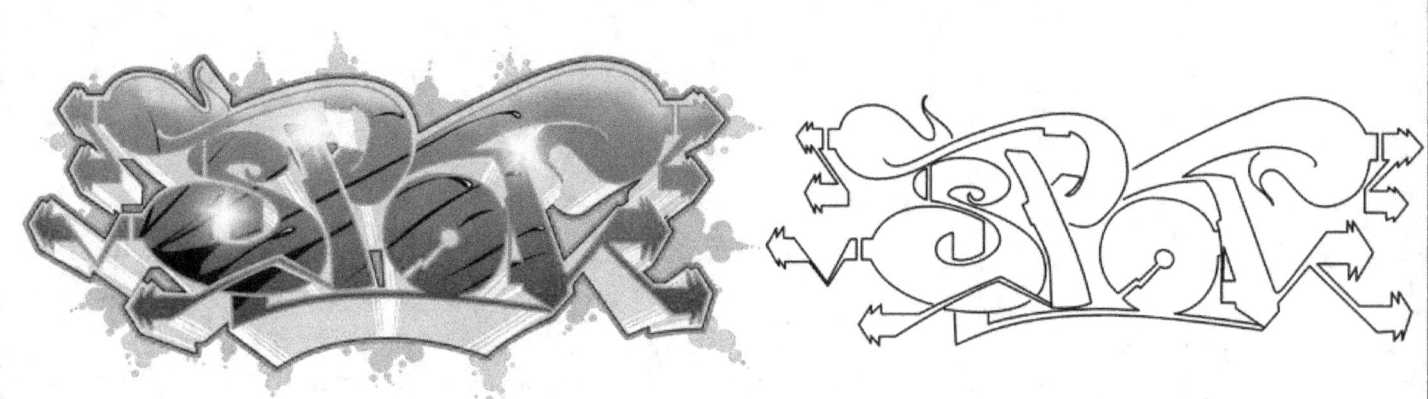

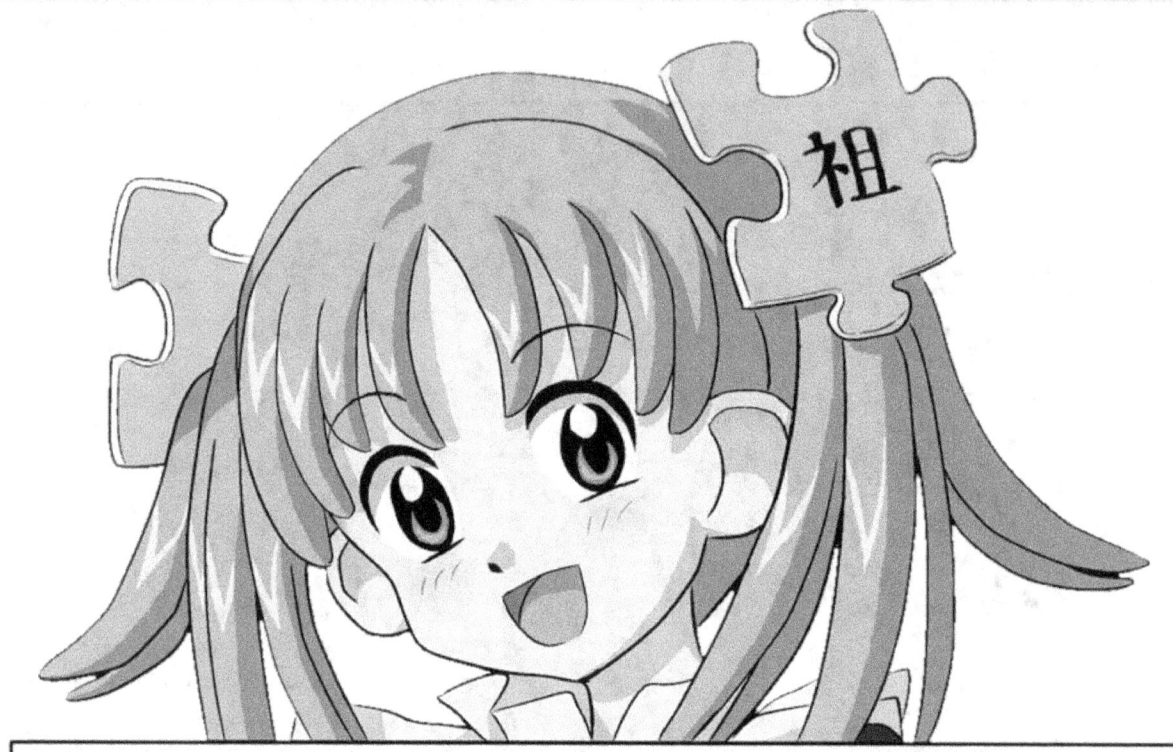

THIS BOOK BELONGS TO:

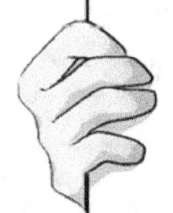

Artist Tools

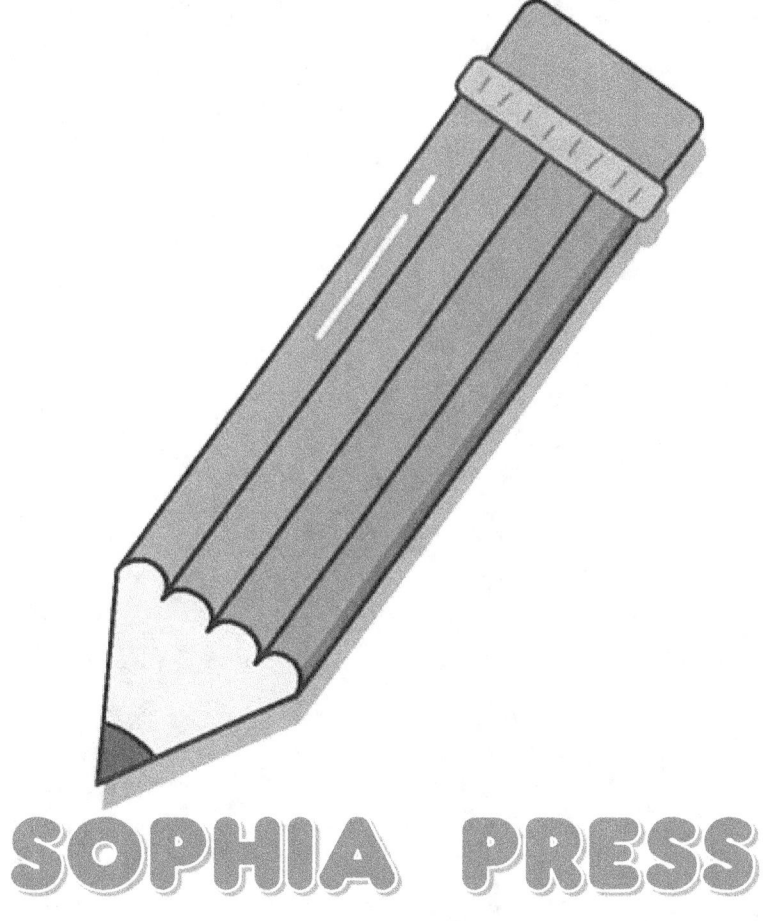

SOPHIA PRESS

ALL YOU NEED: DRAWING PAPERPENCILS, ERASERS, PENCIL SHARPENERS, PENS, COLORED PENCILS.AND

A LOT OF YOUR CREATIVITY

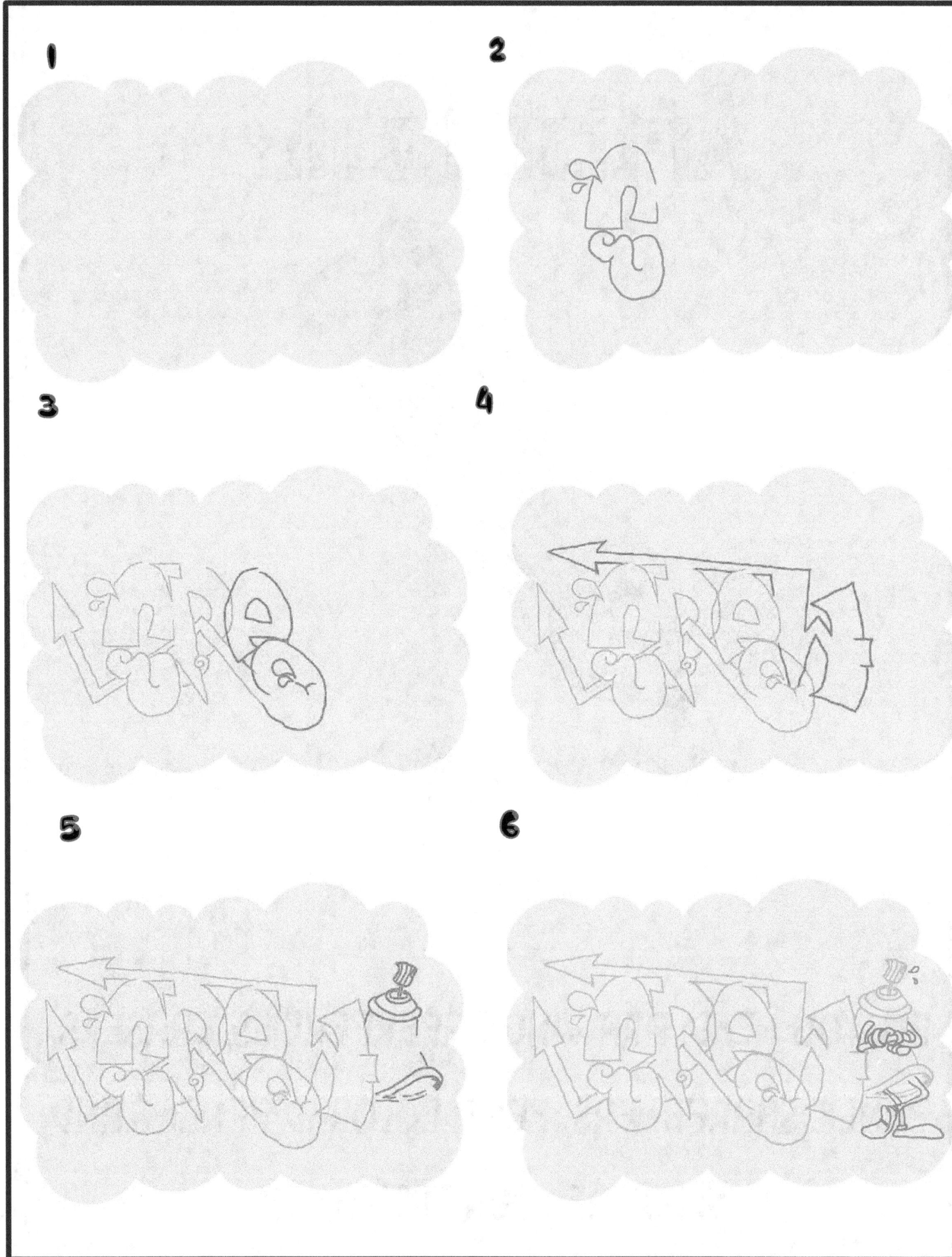

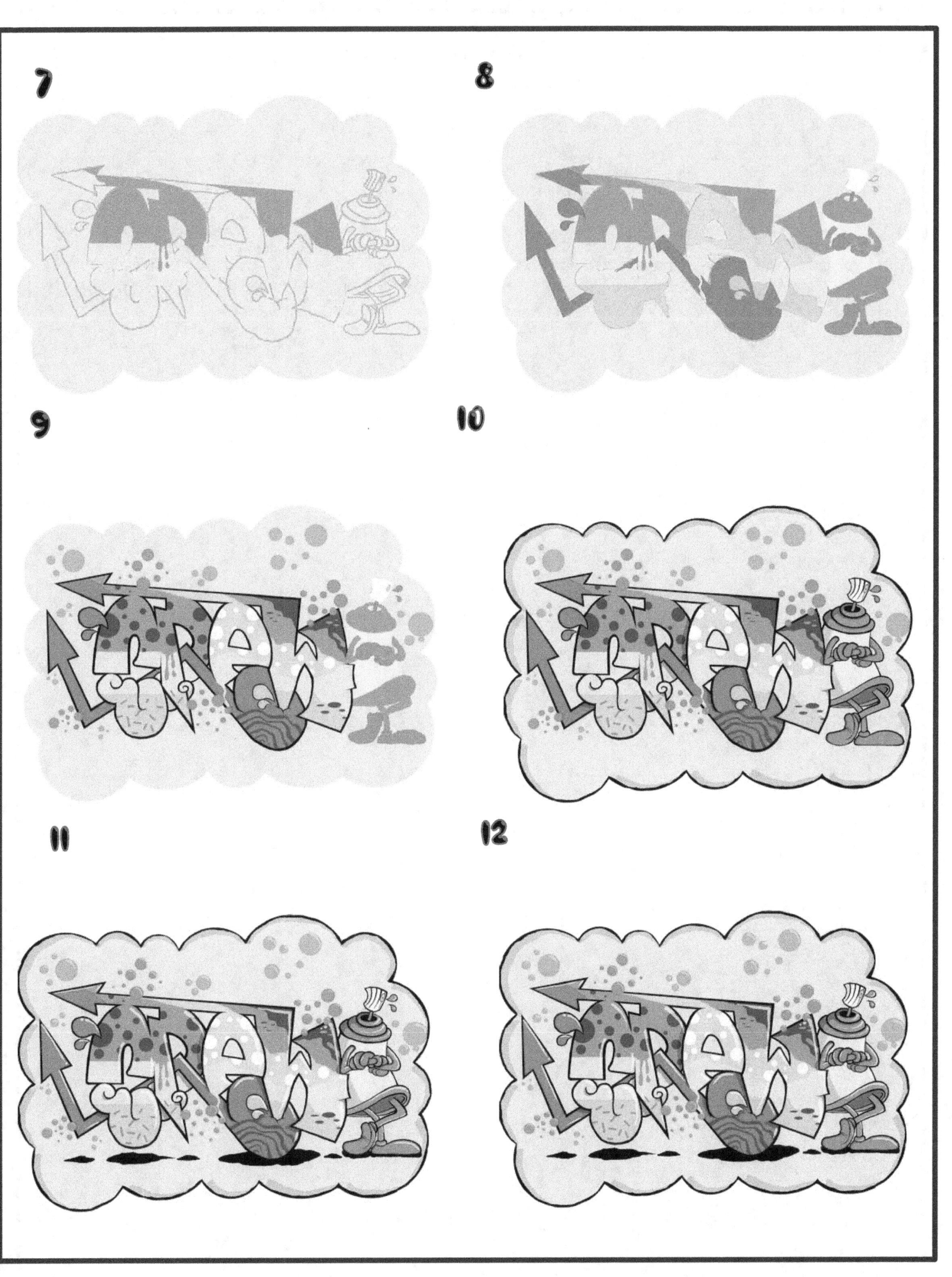

make your own art

1

2

3

4

5

6

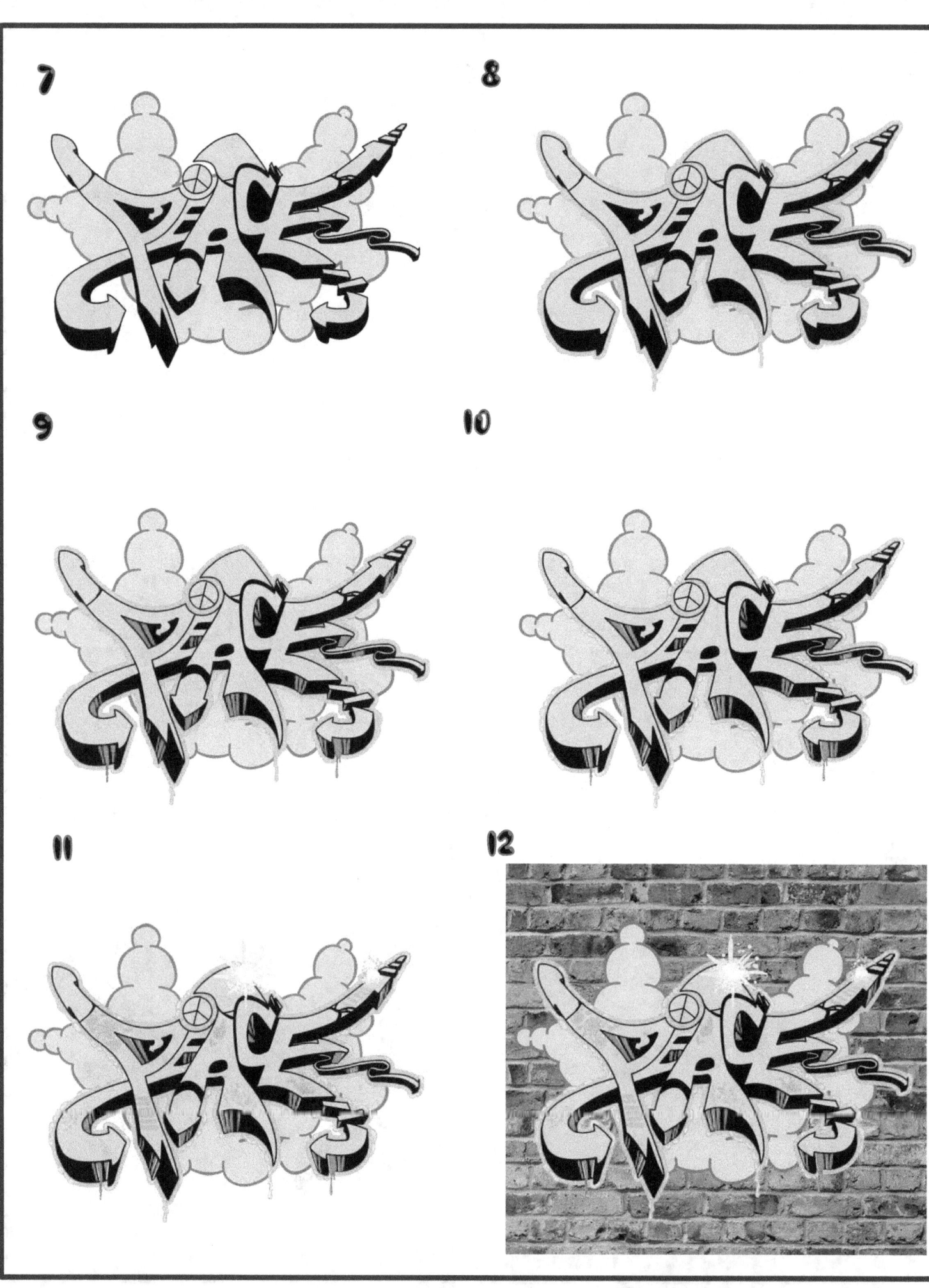

make your own art

1

2

3

4

5

6

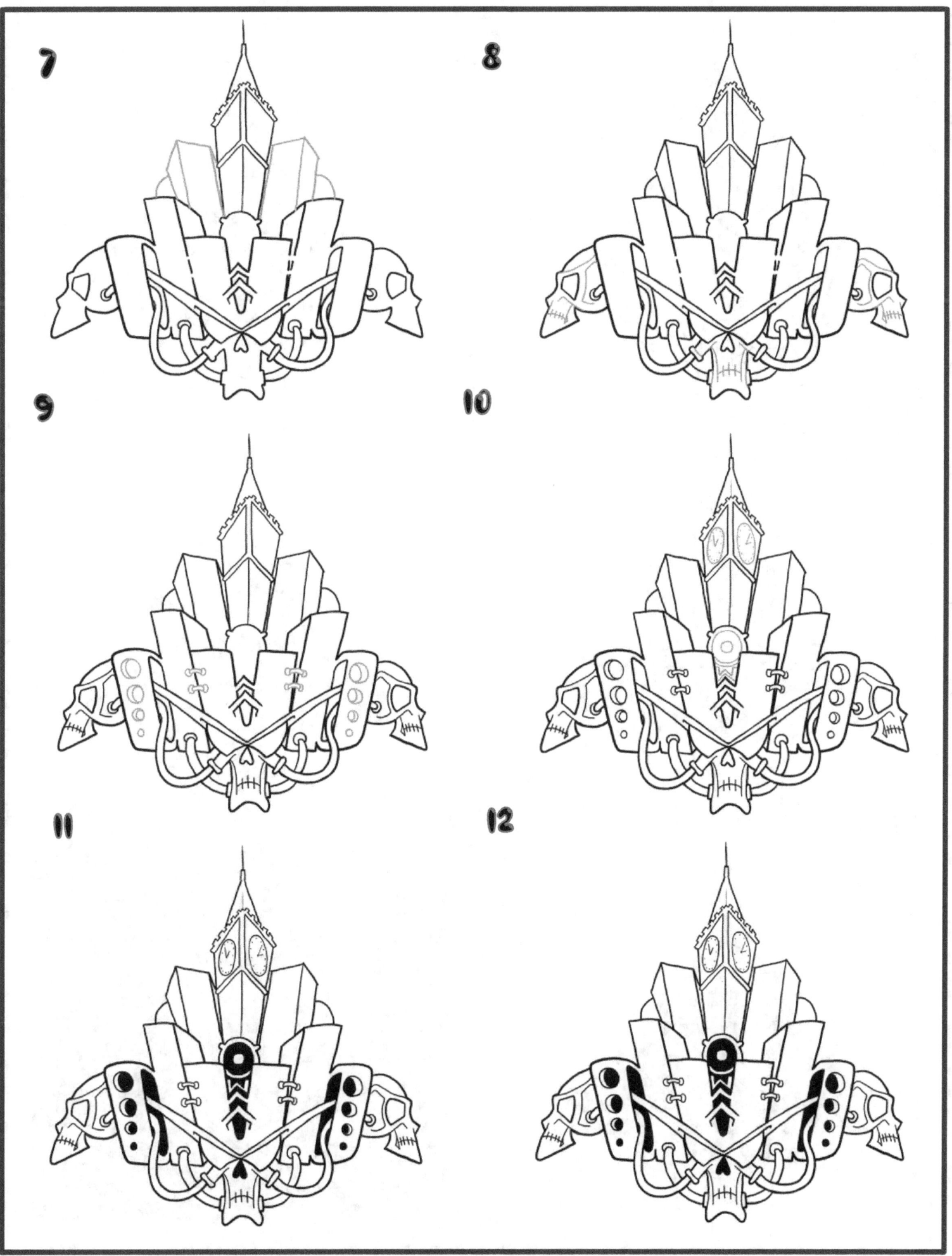

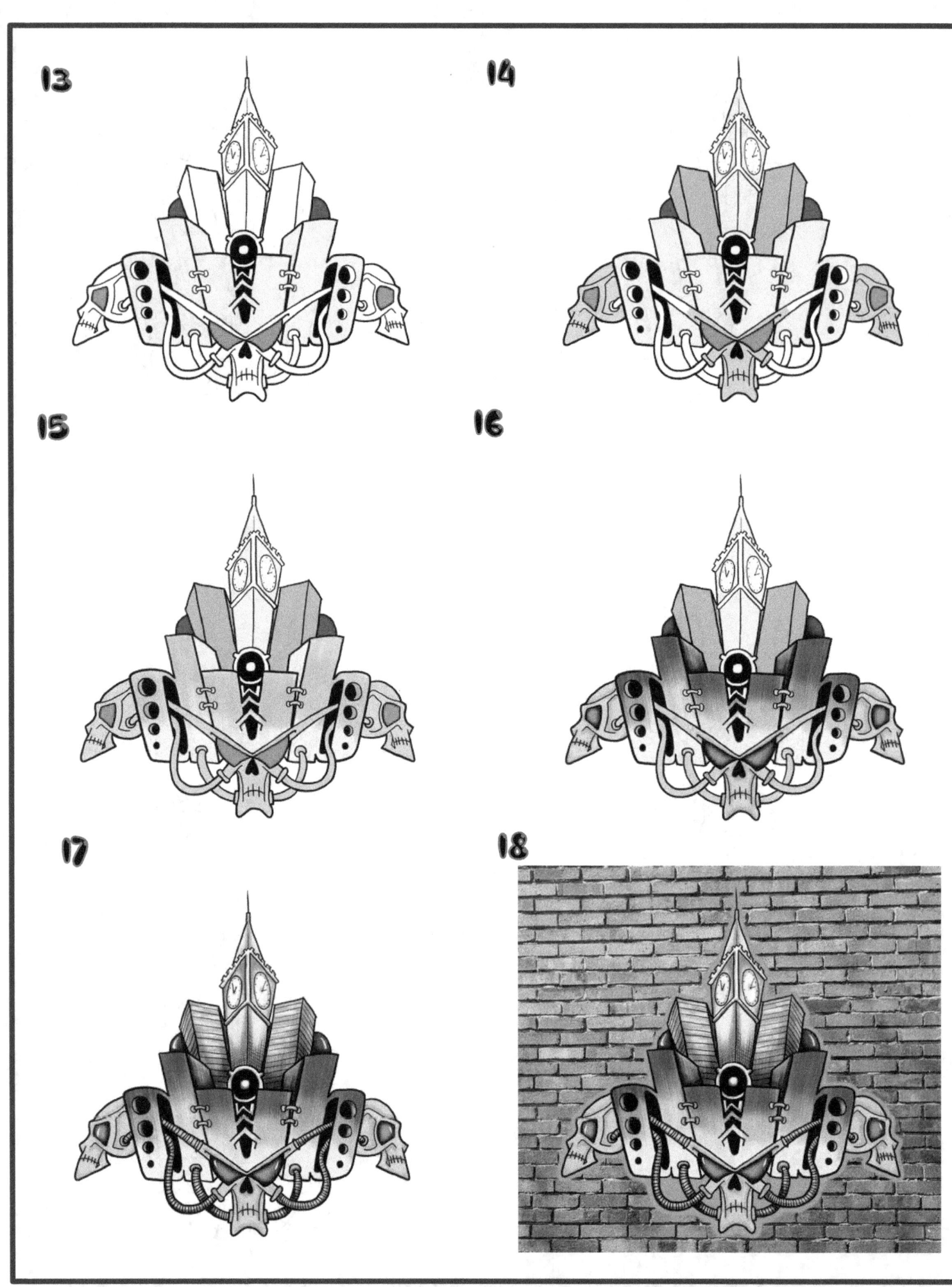

make your own art

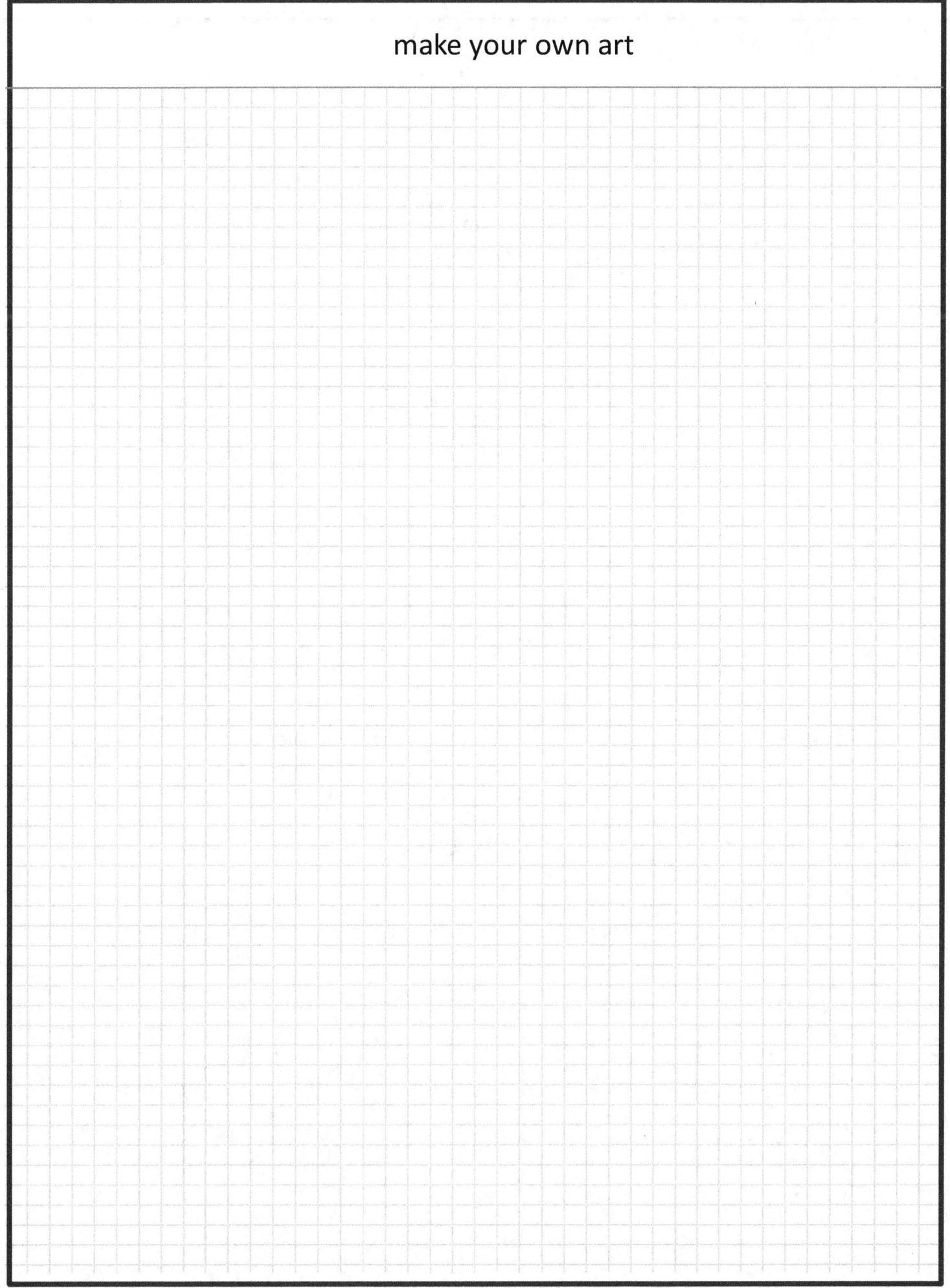

1

2

3

4

5

6

7

8

9

10

11

12

make your own art

make your own art

1

2

3

4

5

6

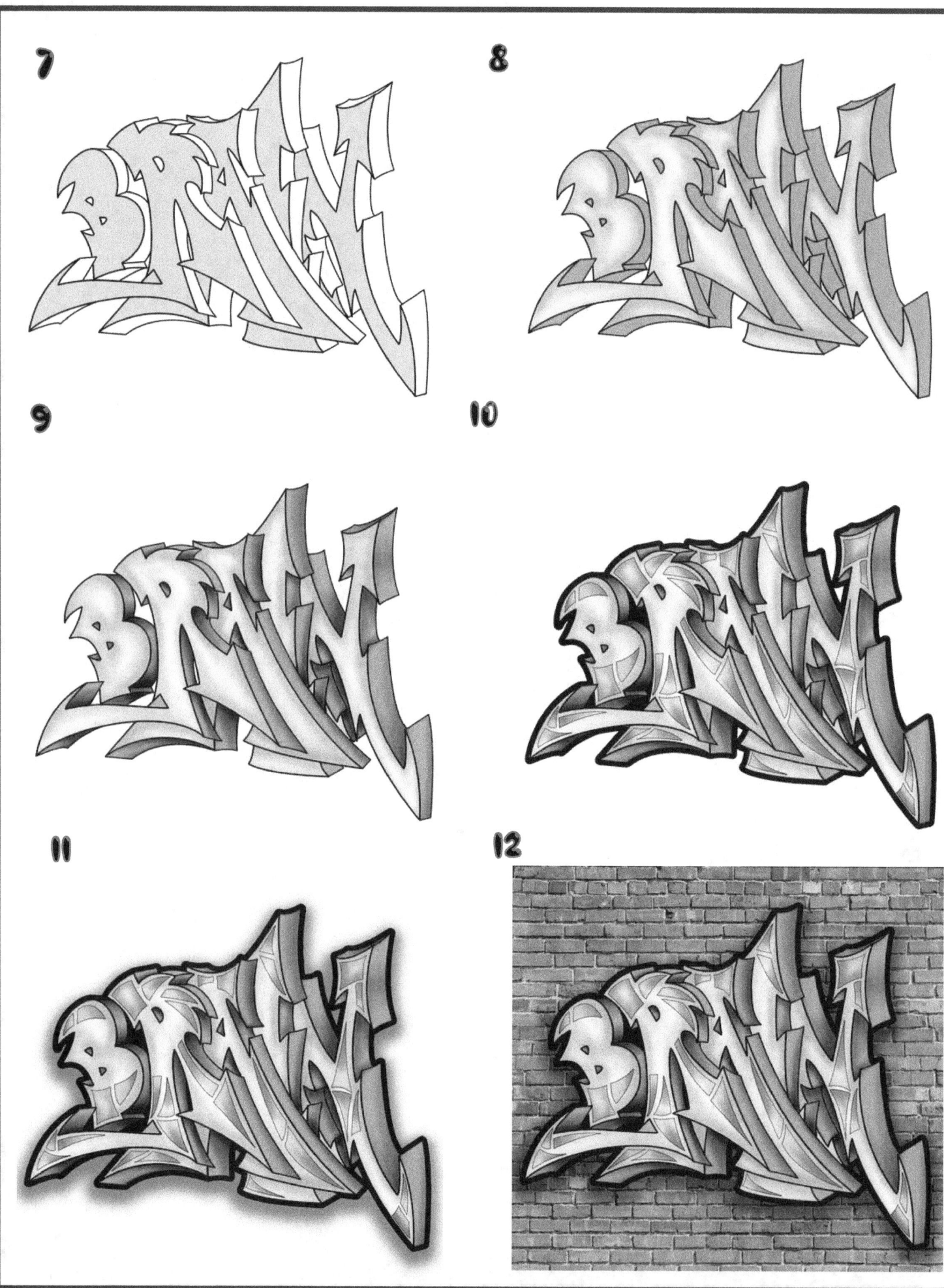

make your own art

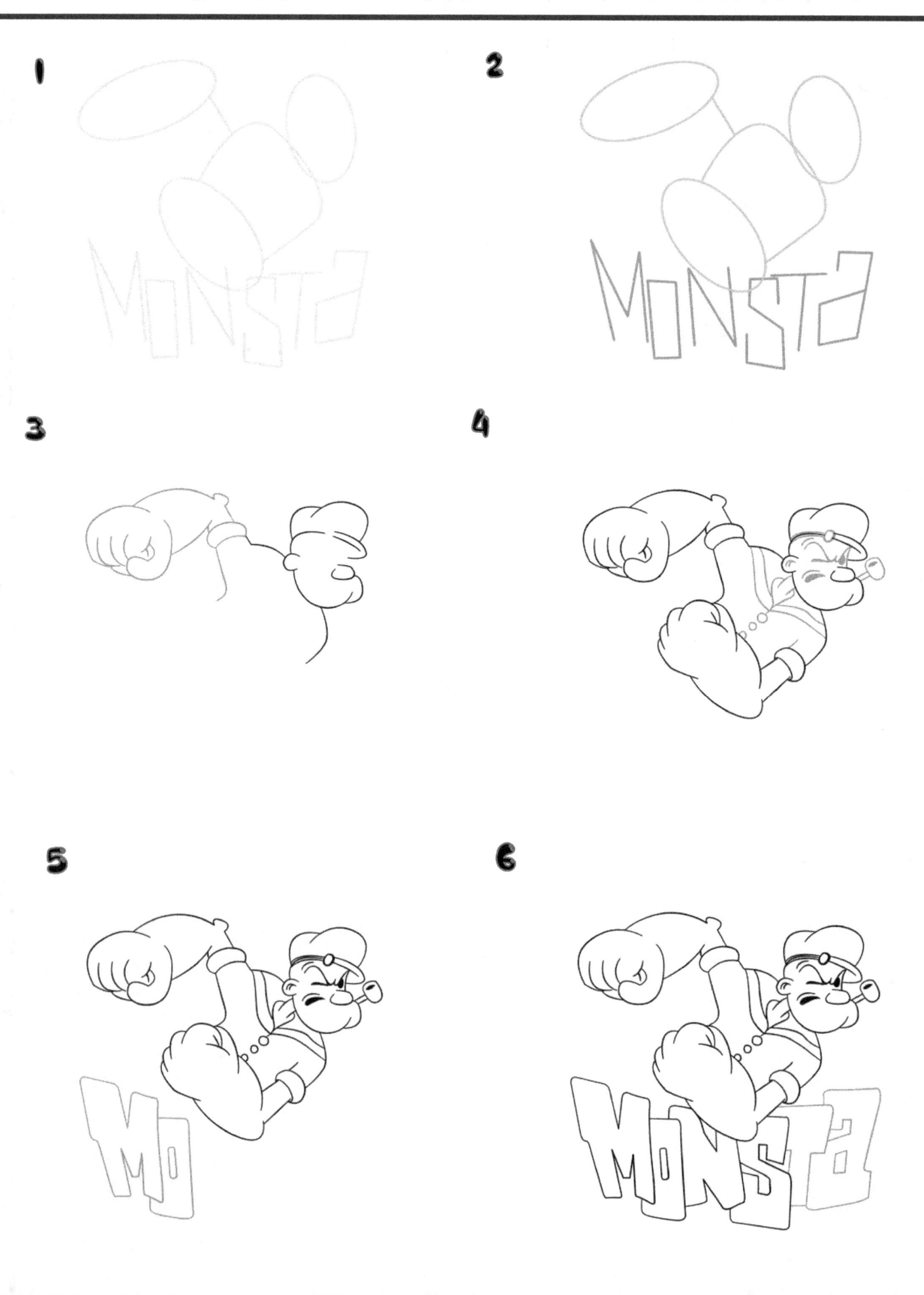

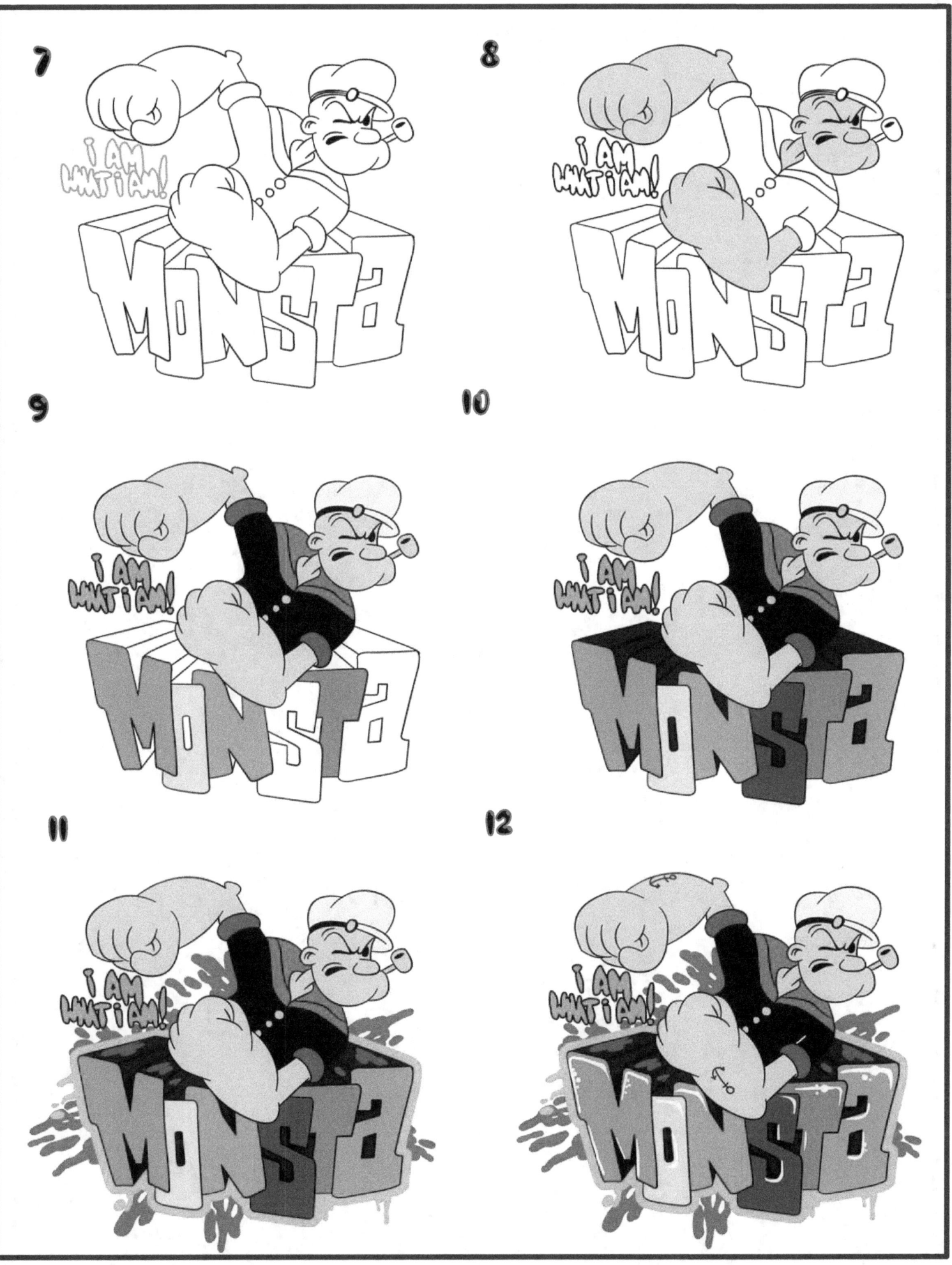

make your own art

1

2

3

4

5

6

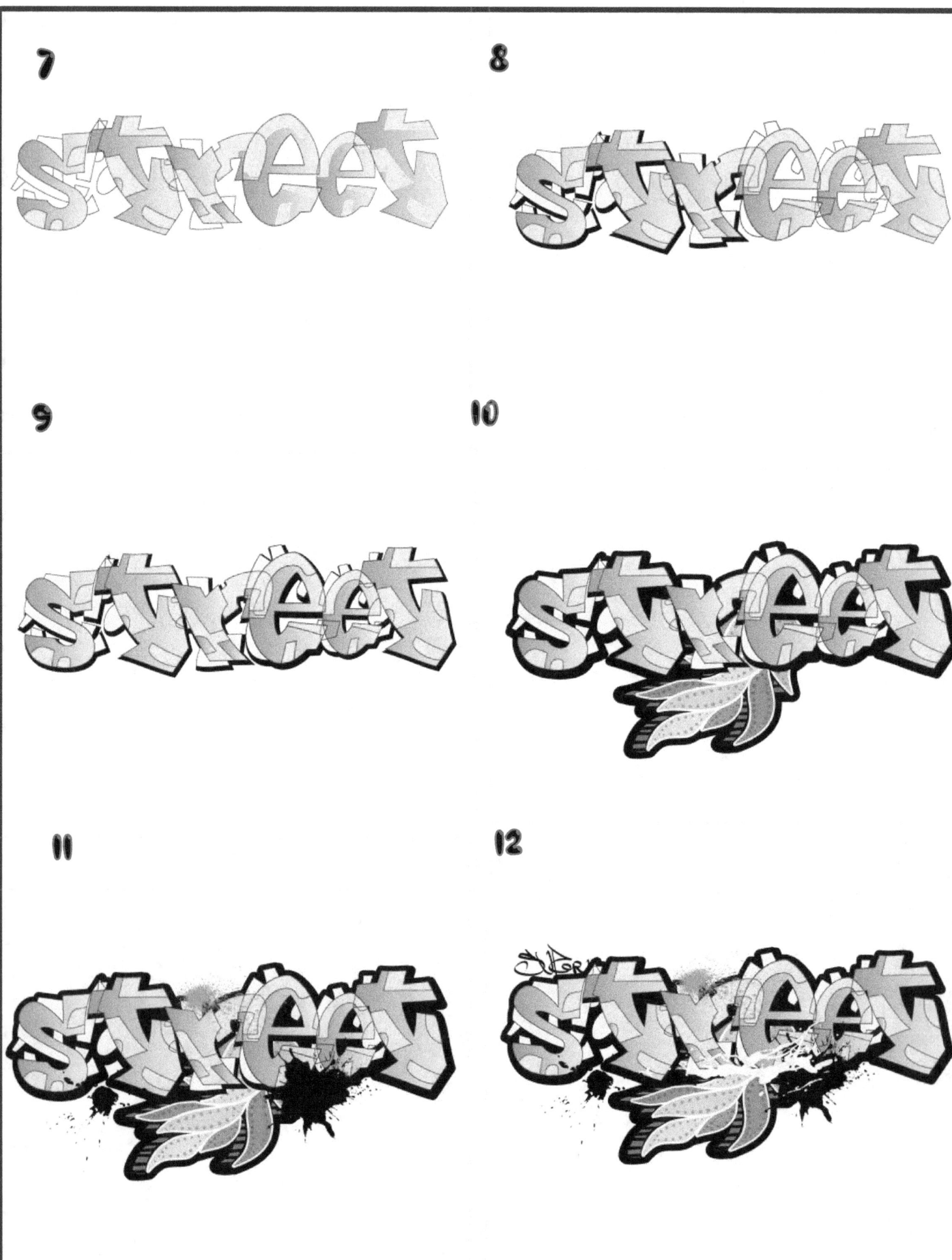

make your own art

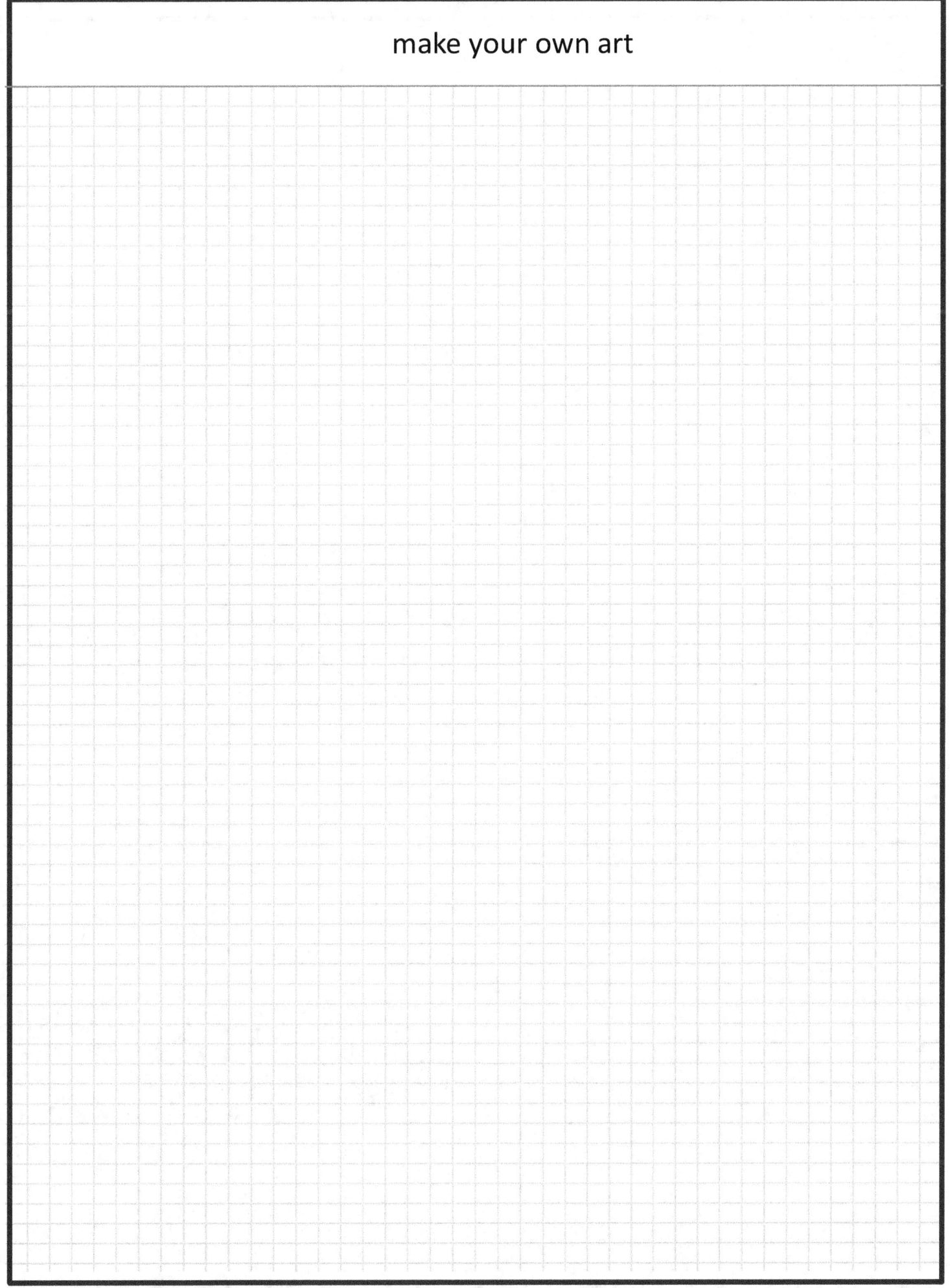

1

2

3

4

5

6

7

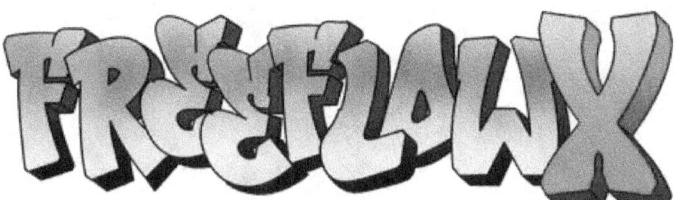

8

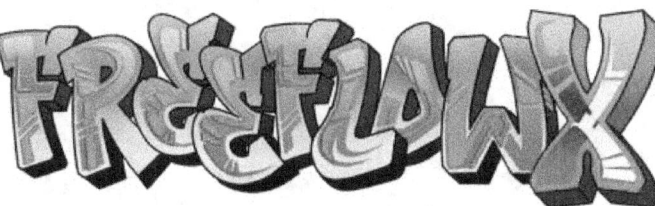

9

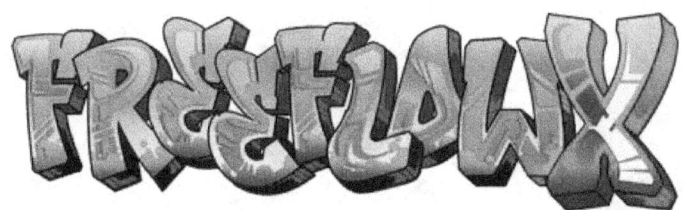

10

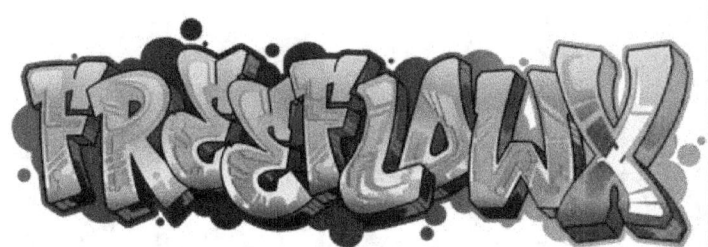

11

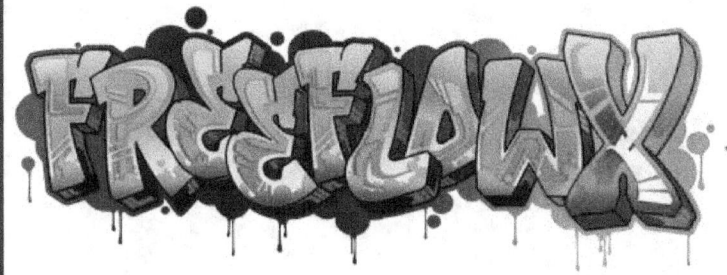

12

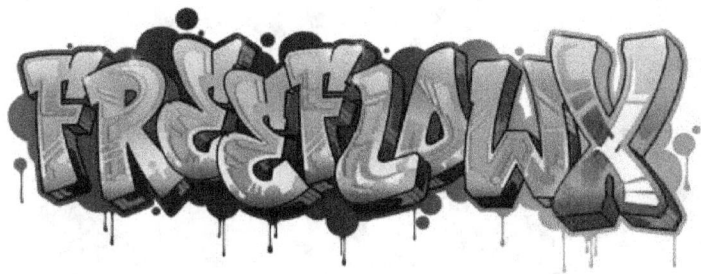

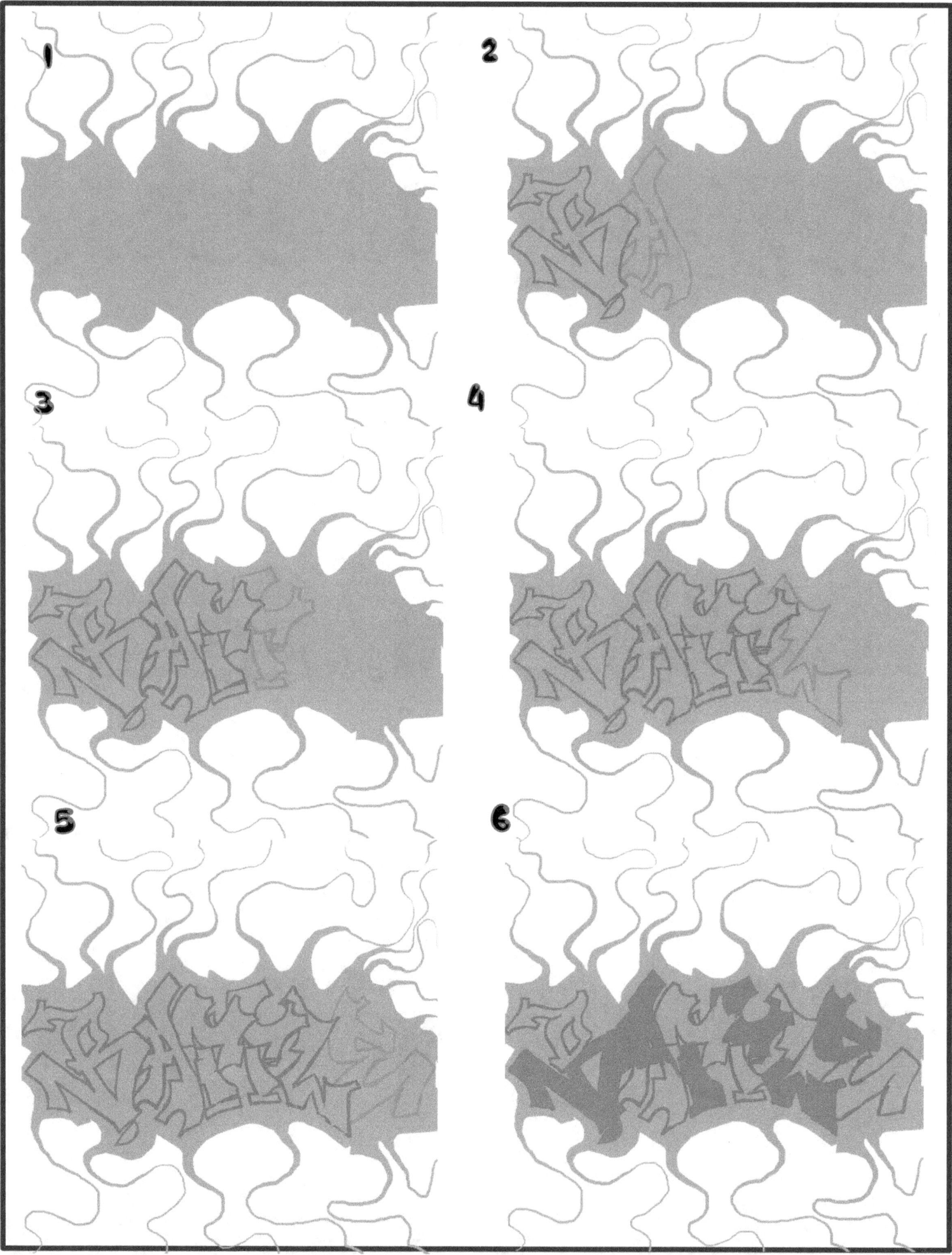

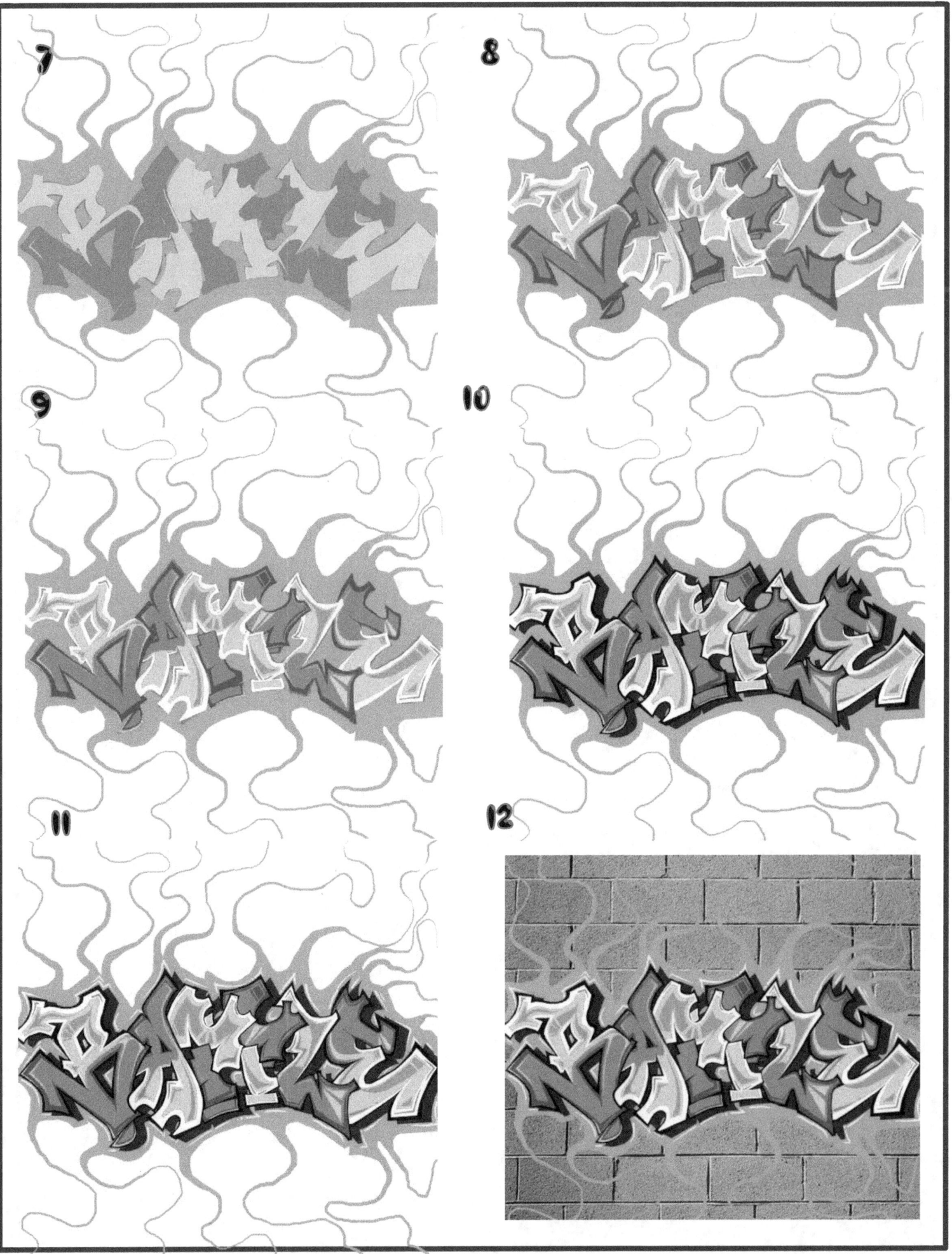

make your own art

make your own art

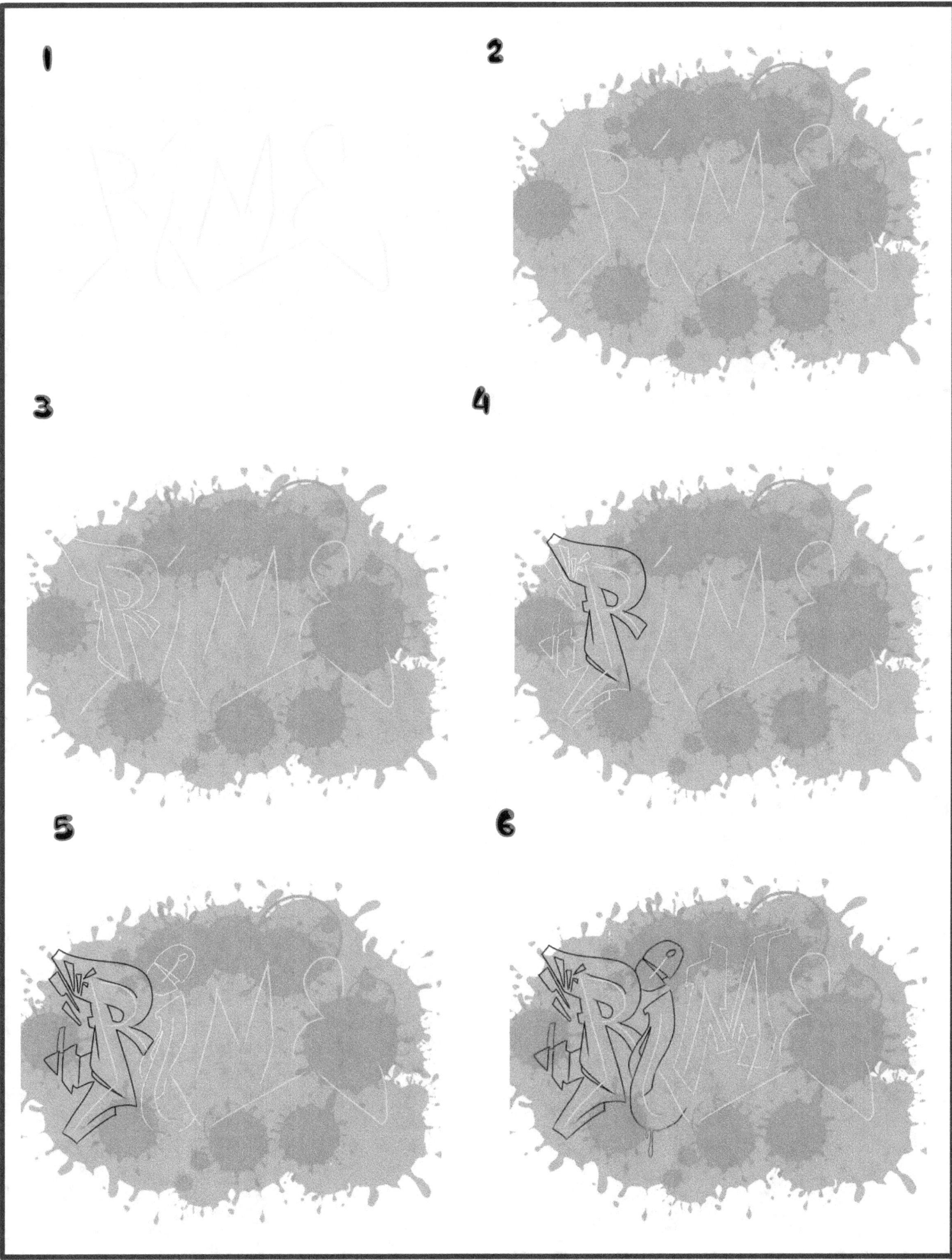

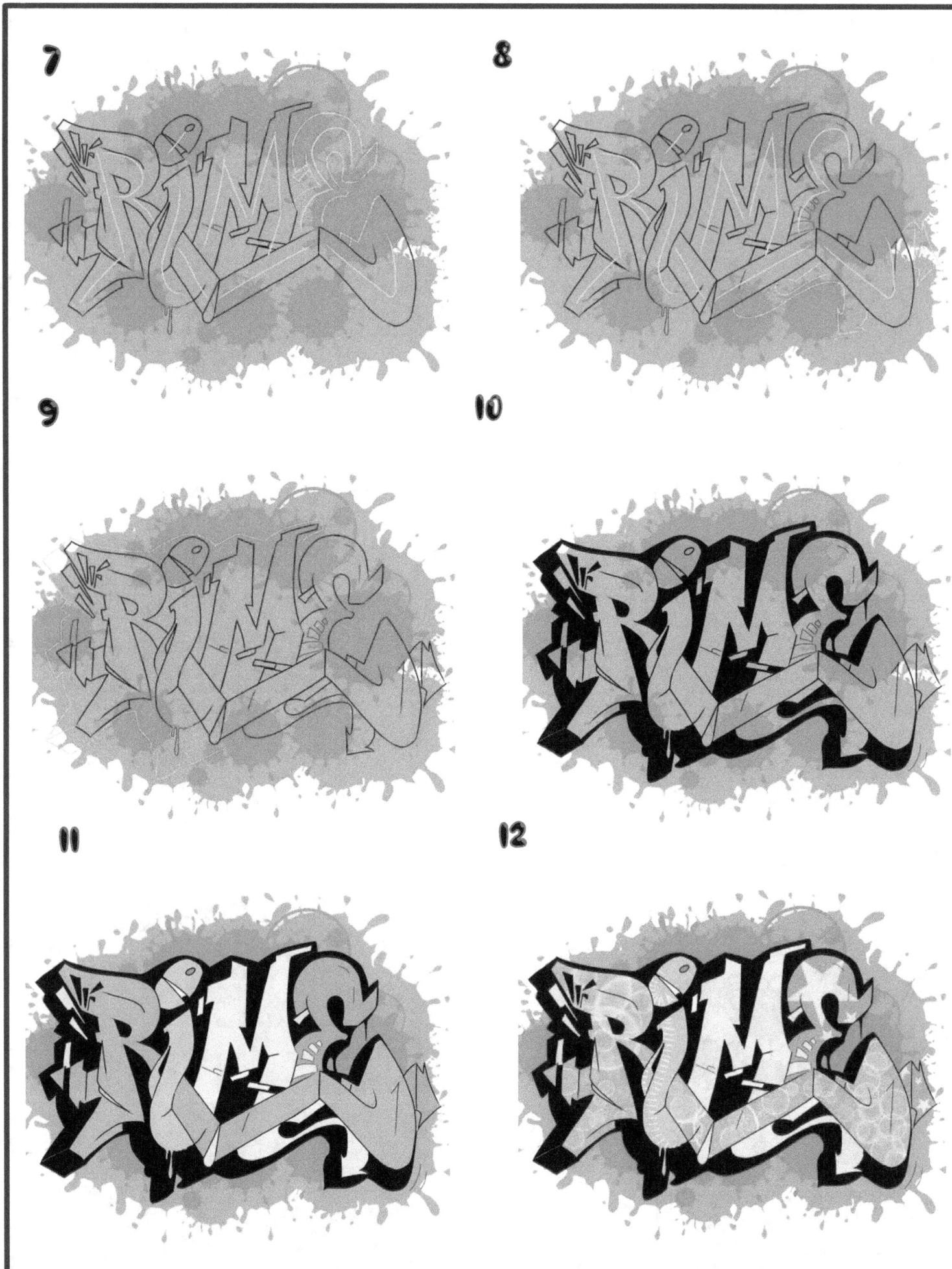

make your own art

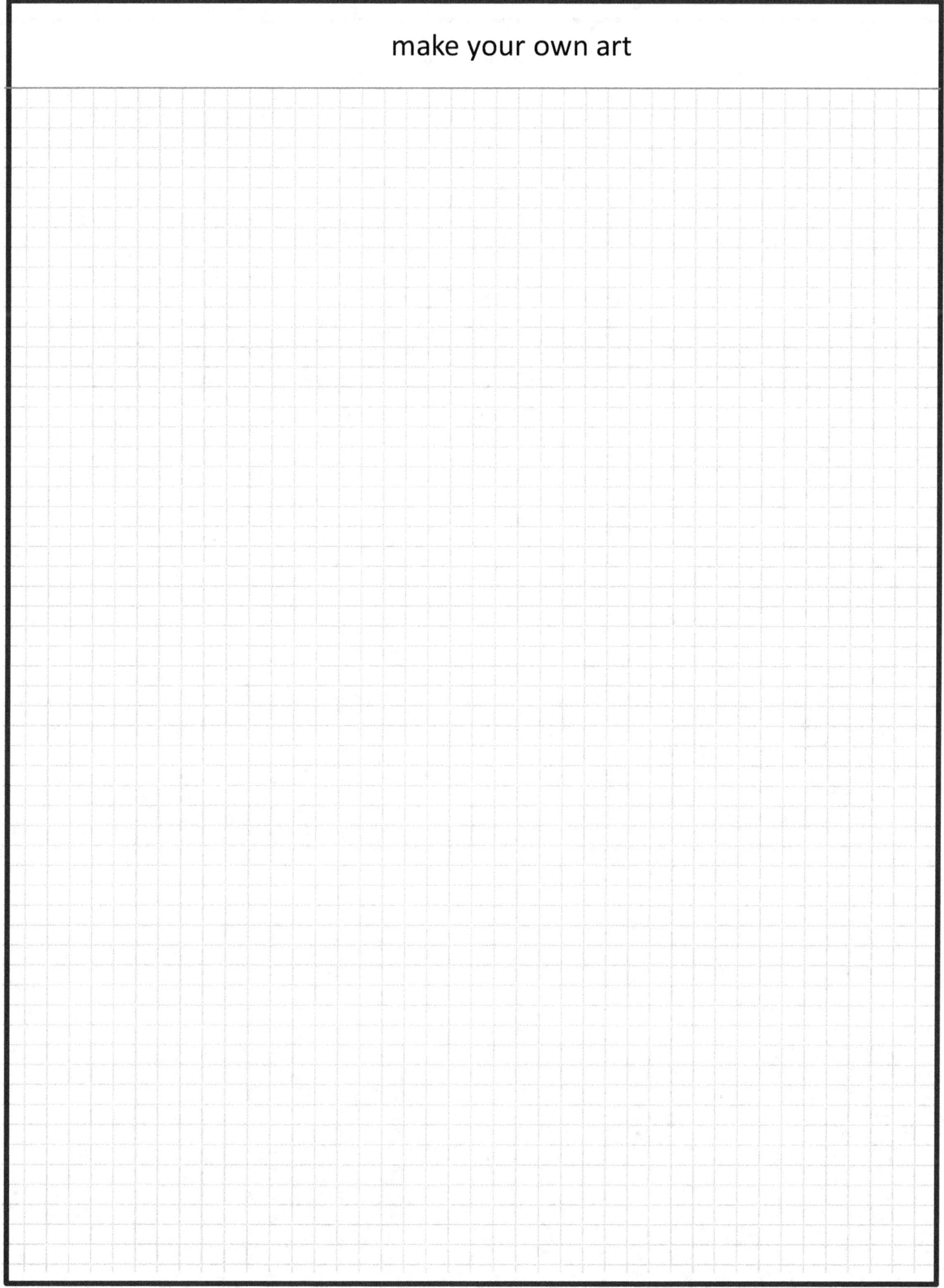

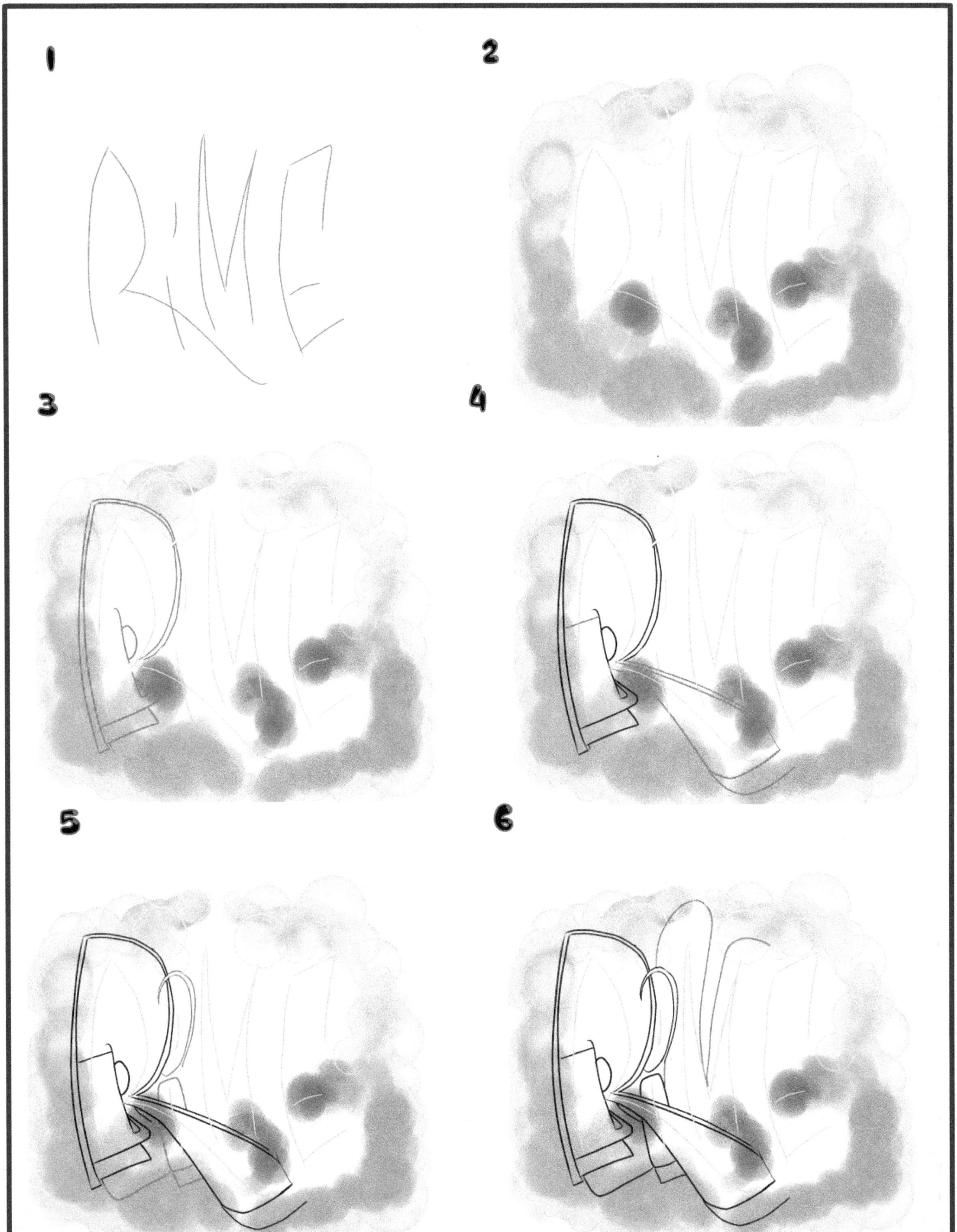
1
2
3
4
5
6

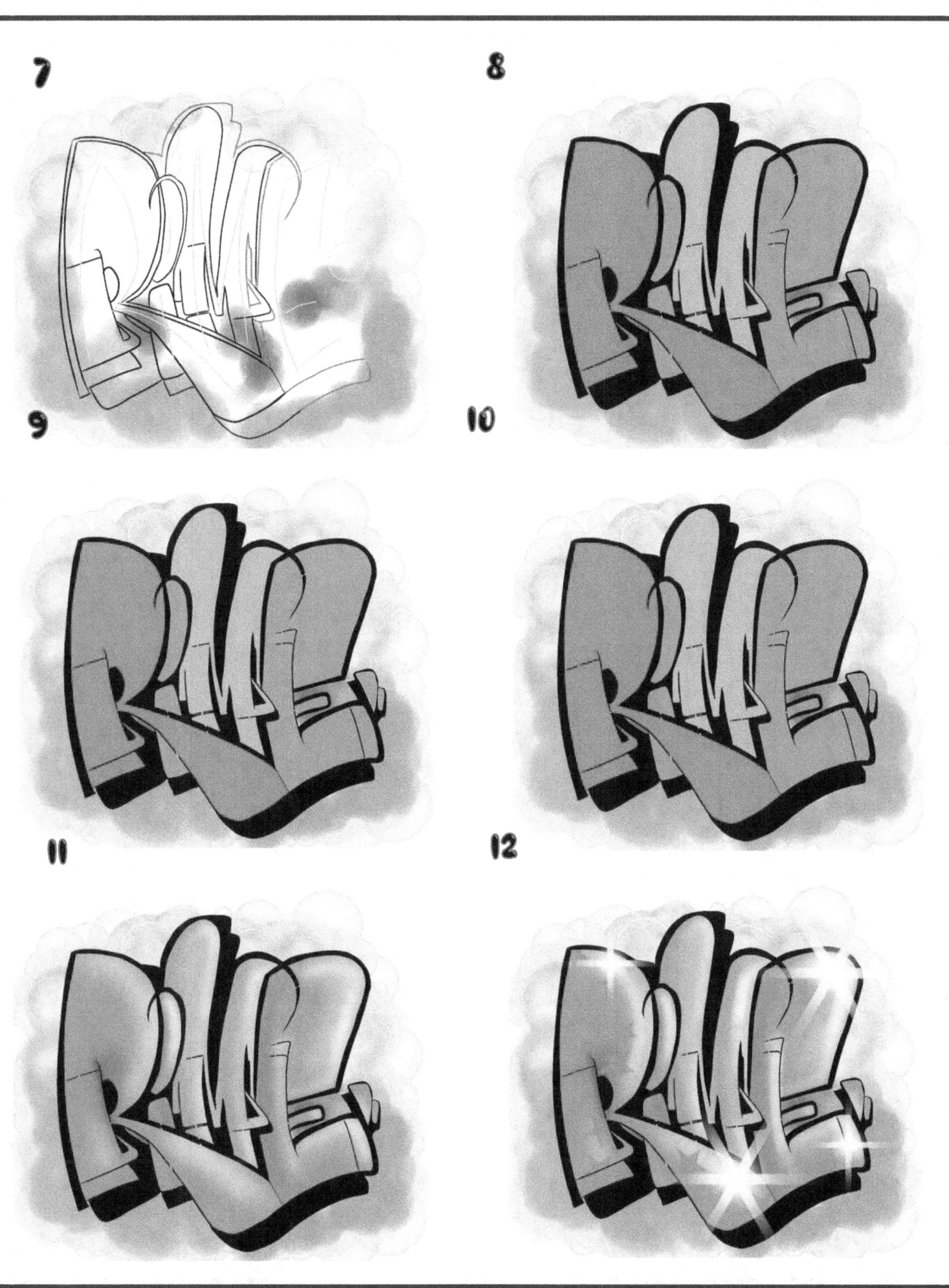

make your own art

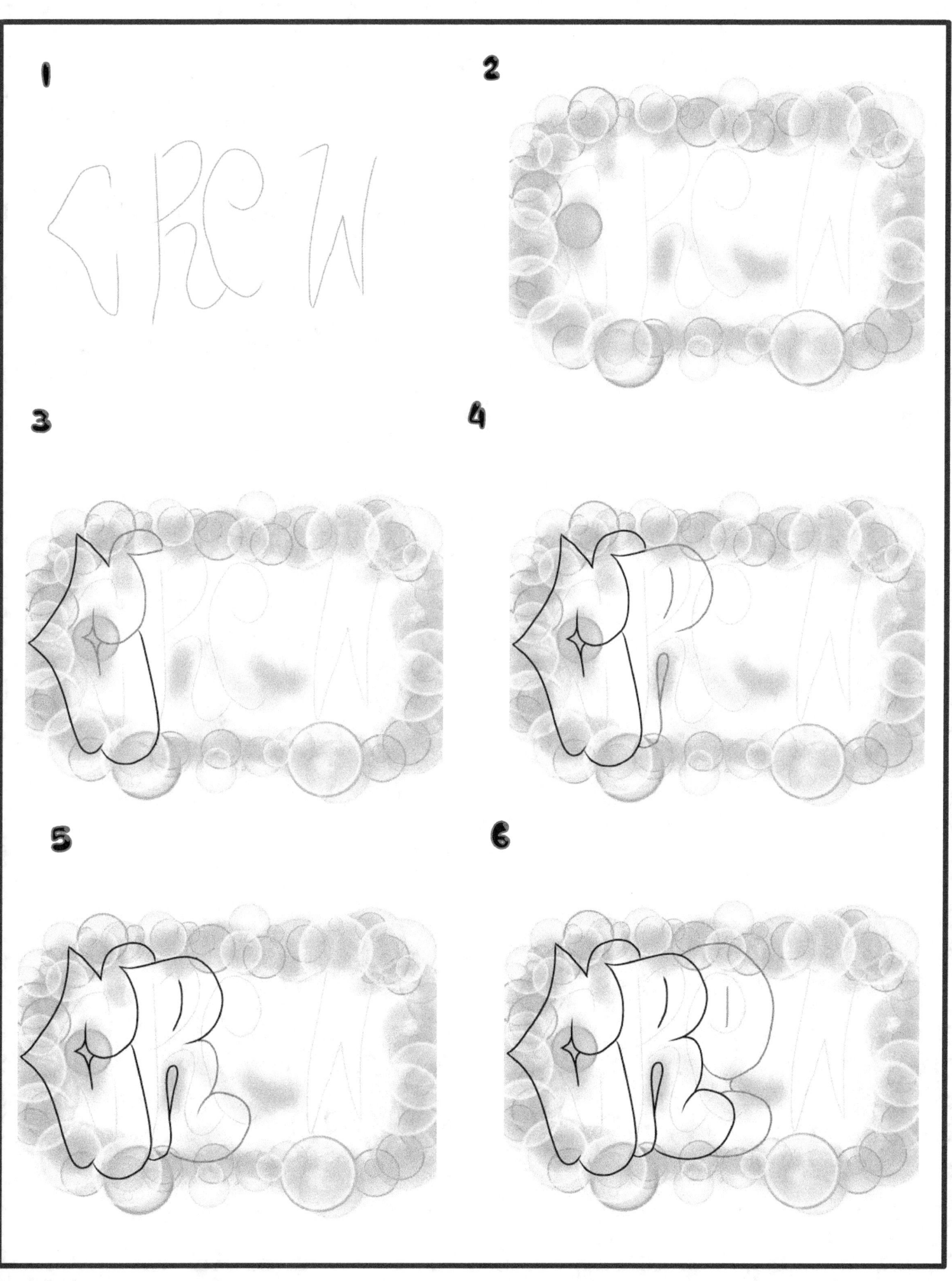

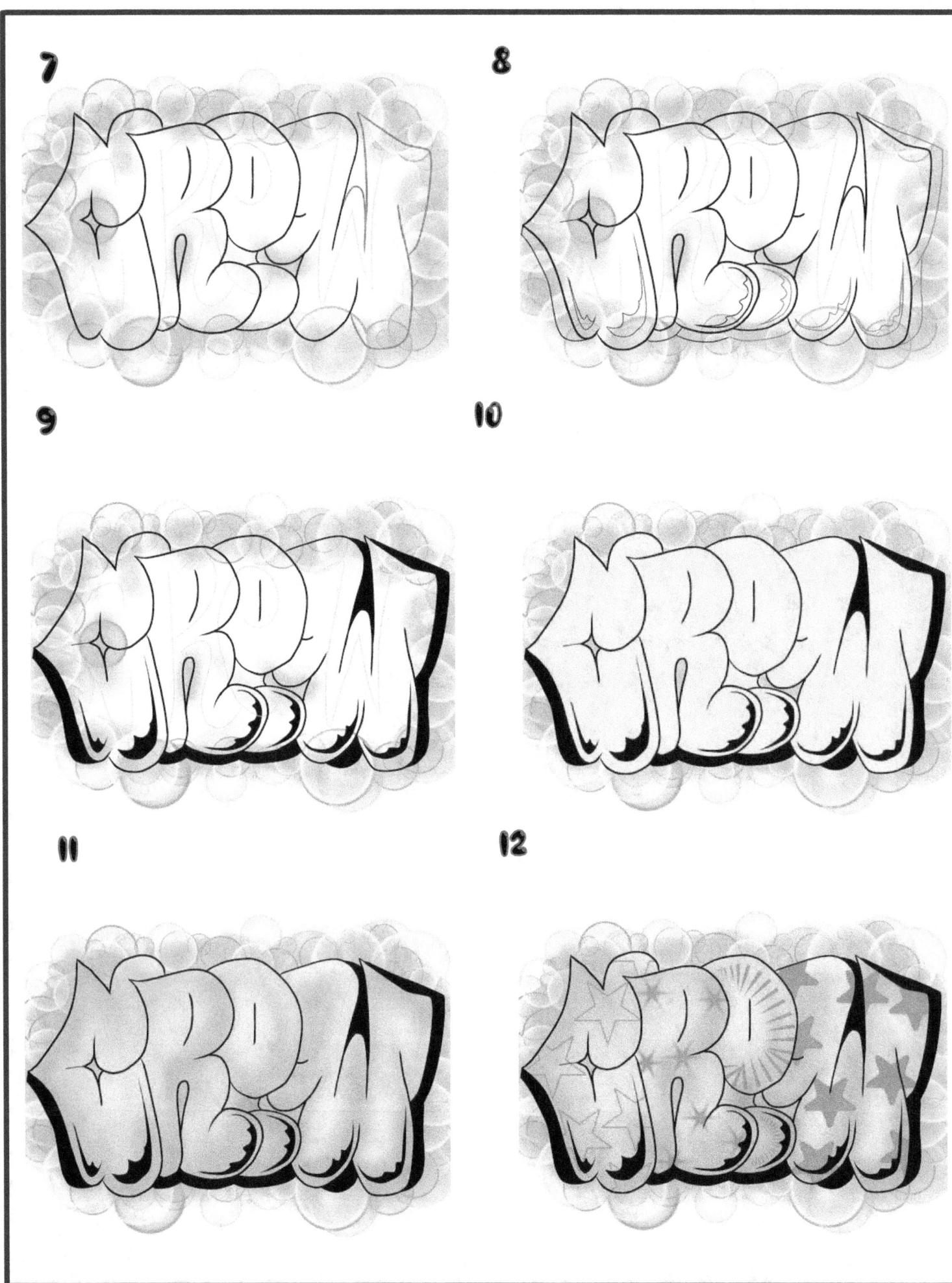

make your own art

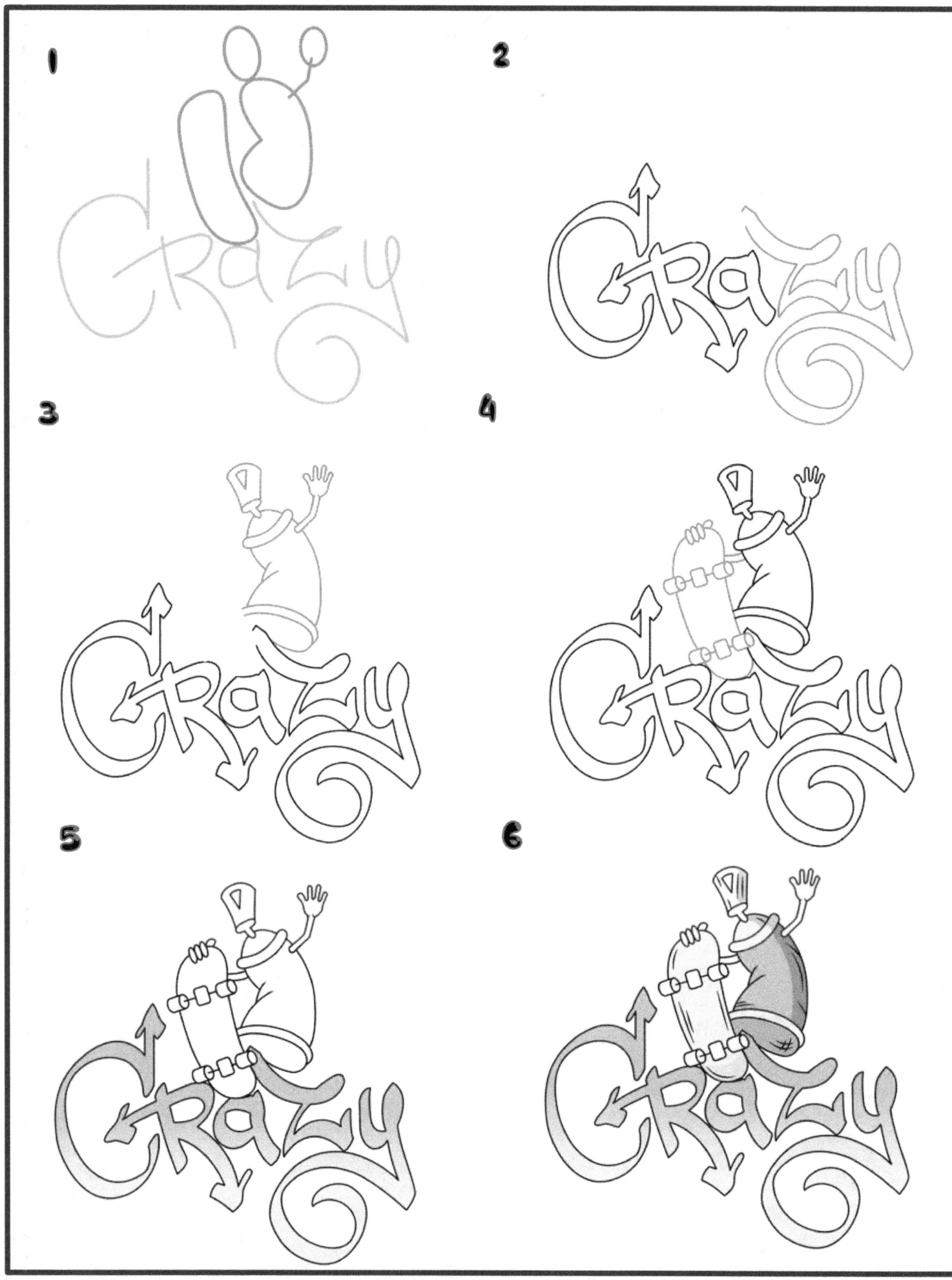

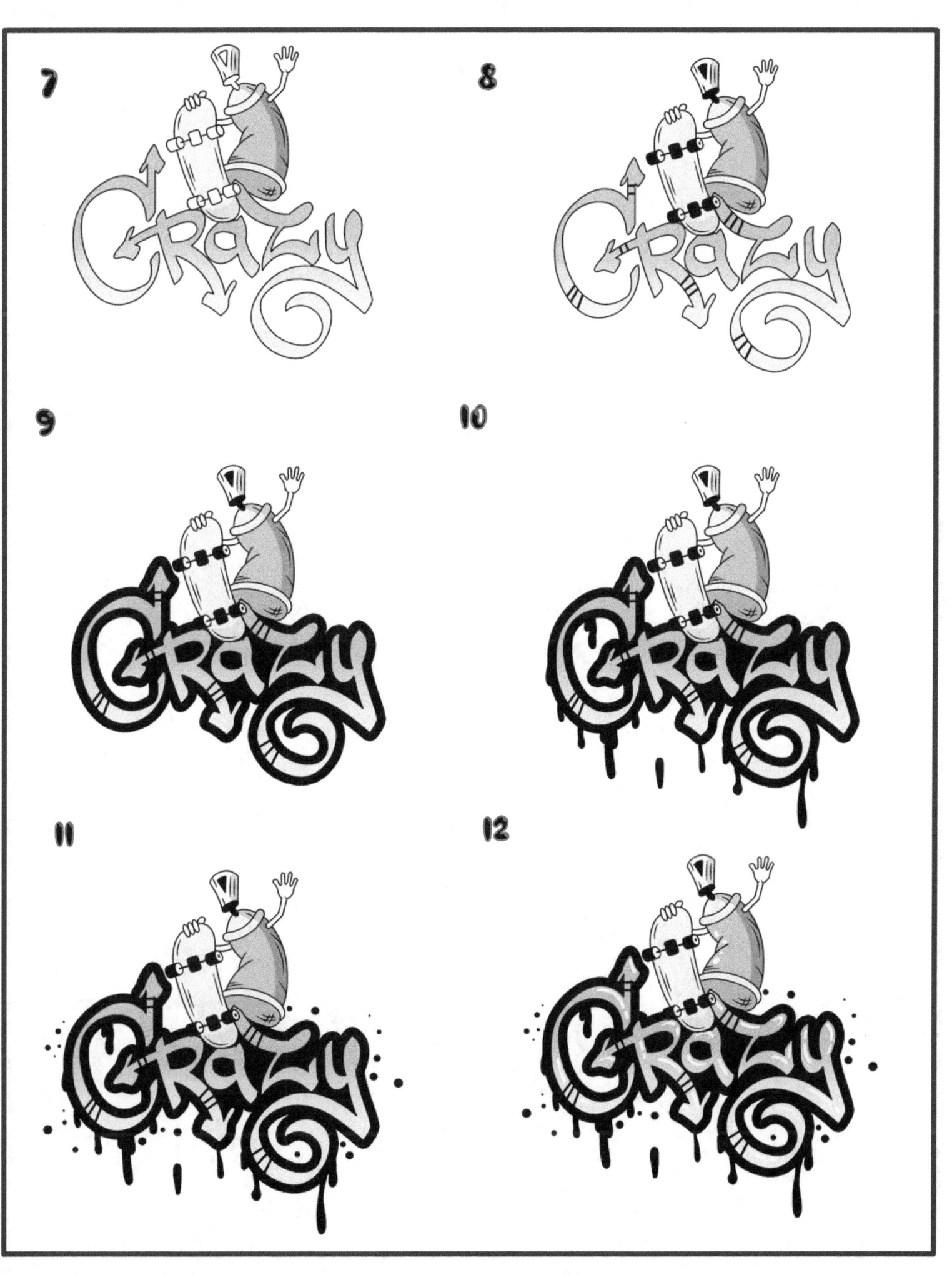

1

2

3

4

5

6

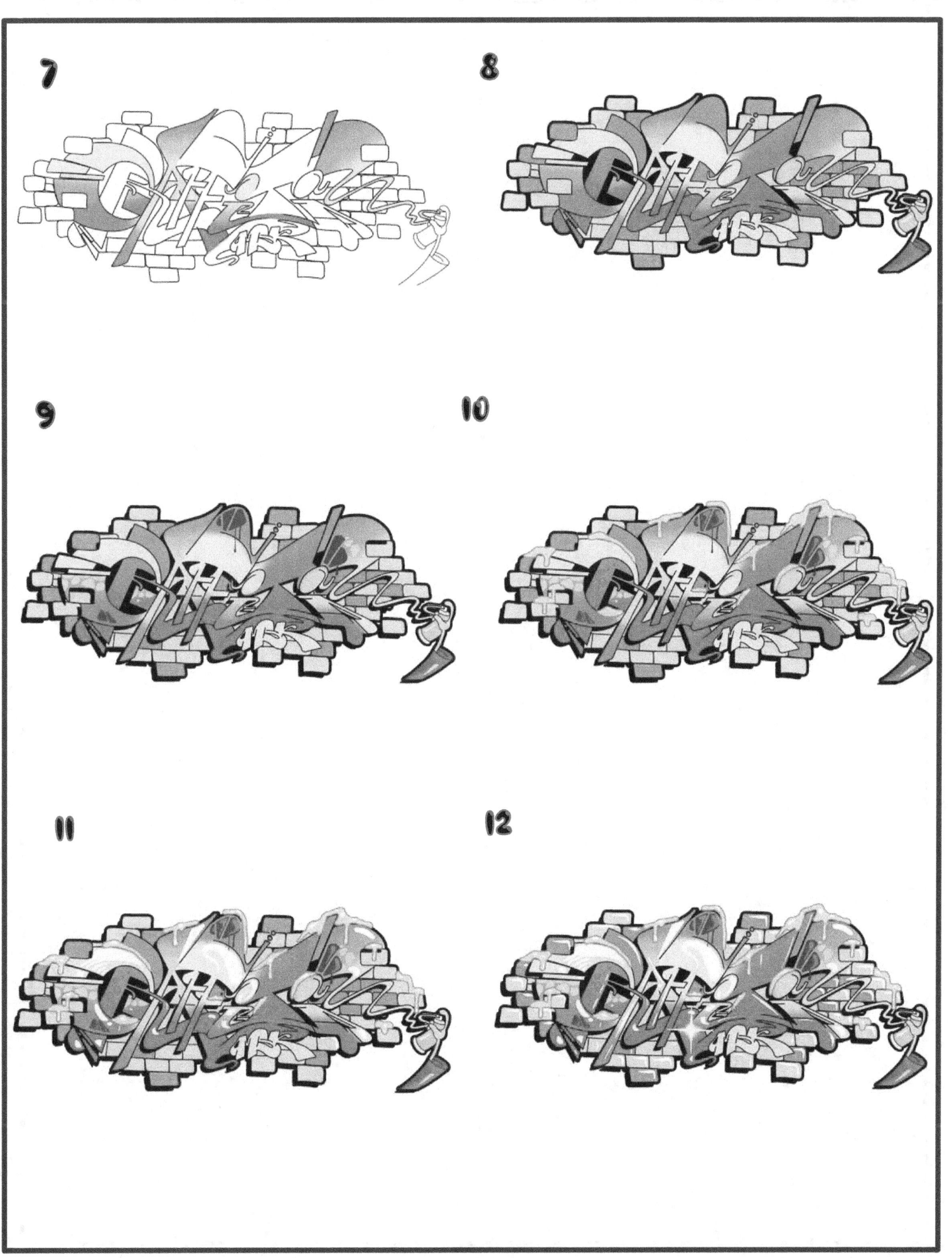

make your own art

1

2

3

4

5

6

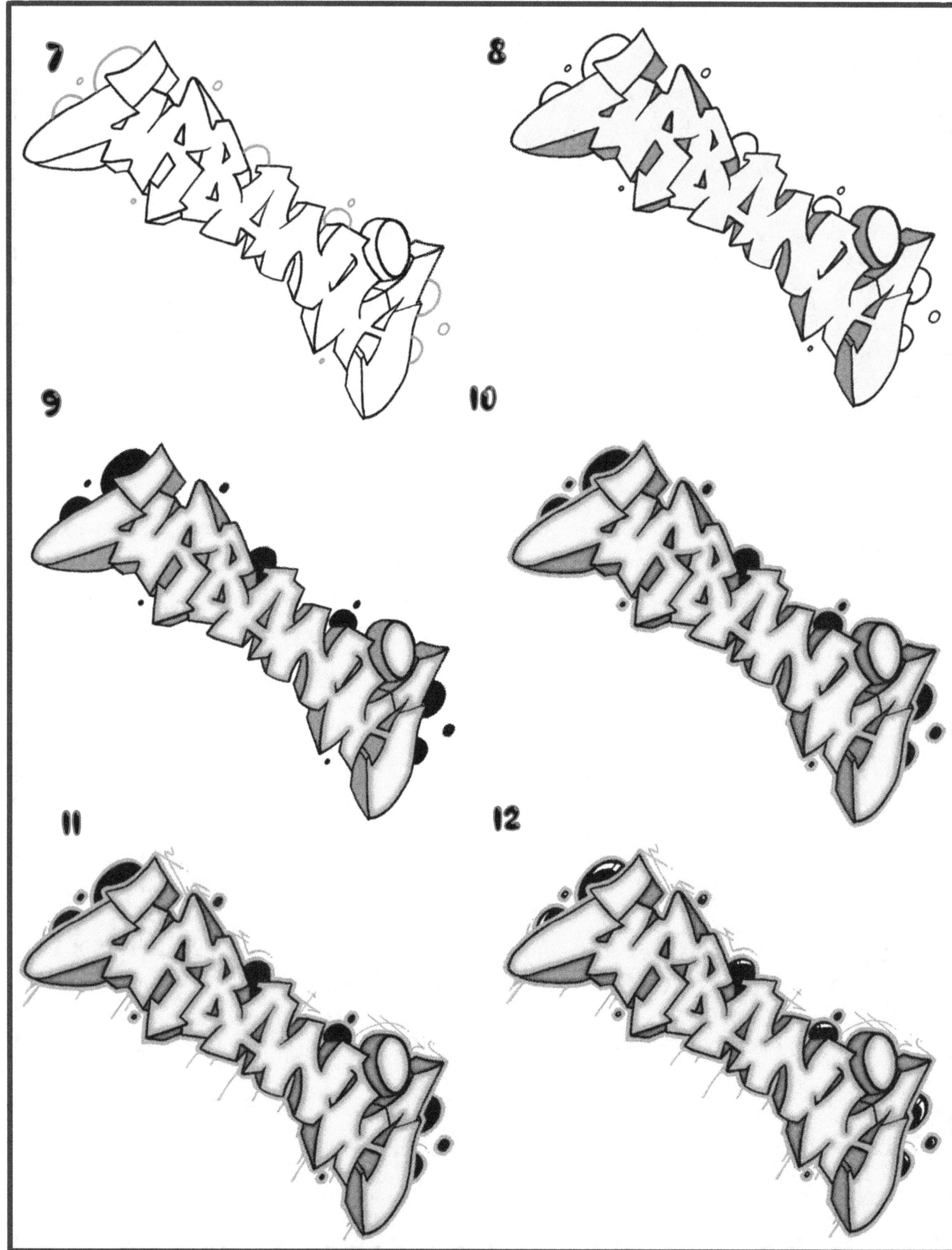

make your own art

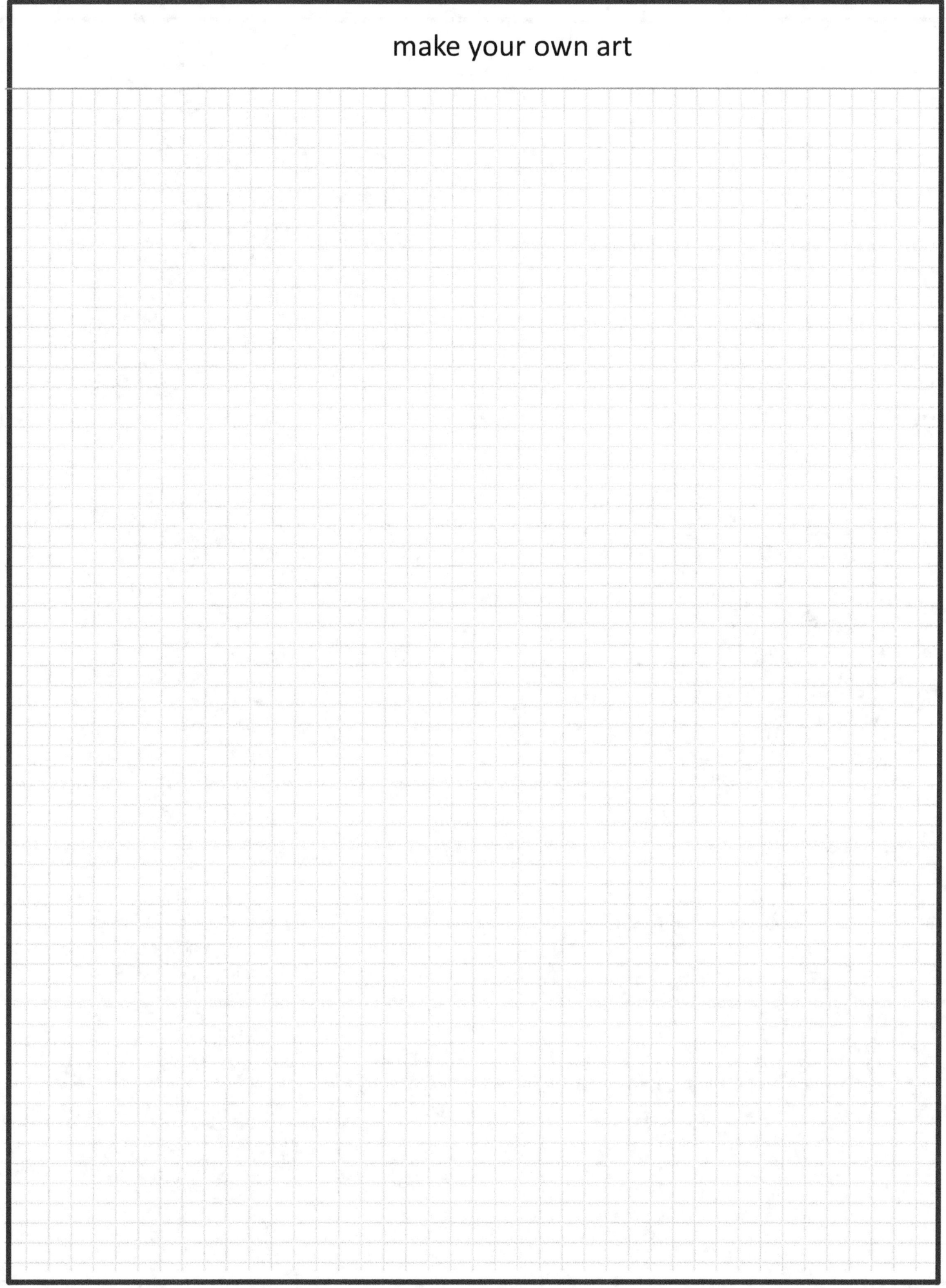

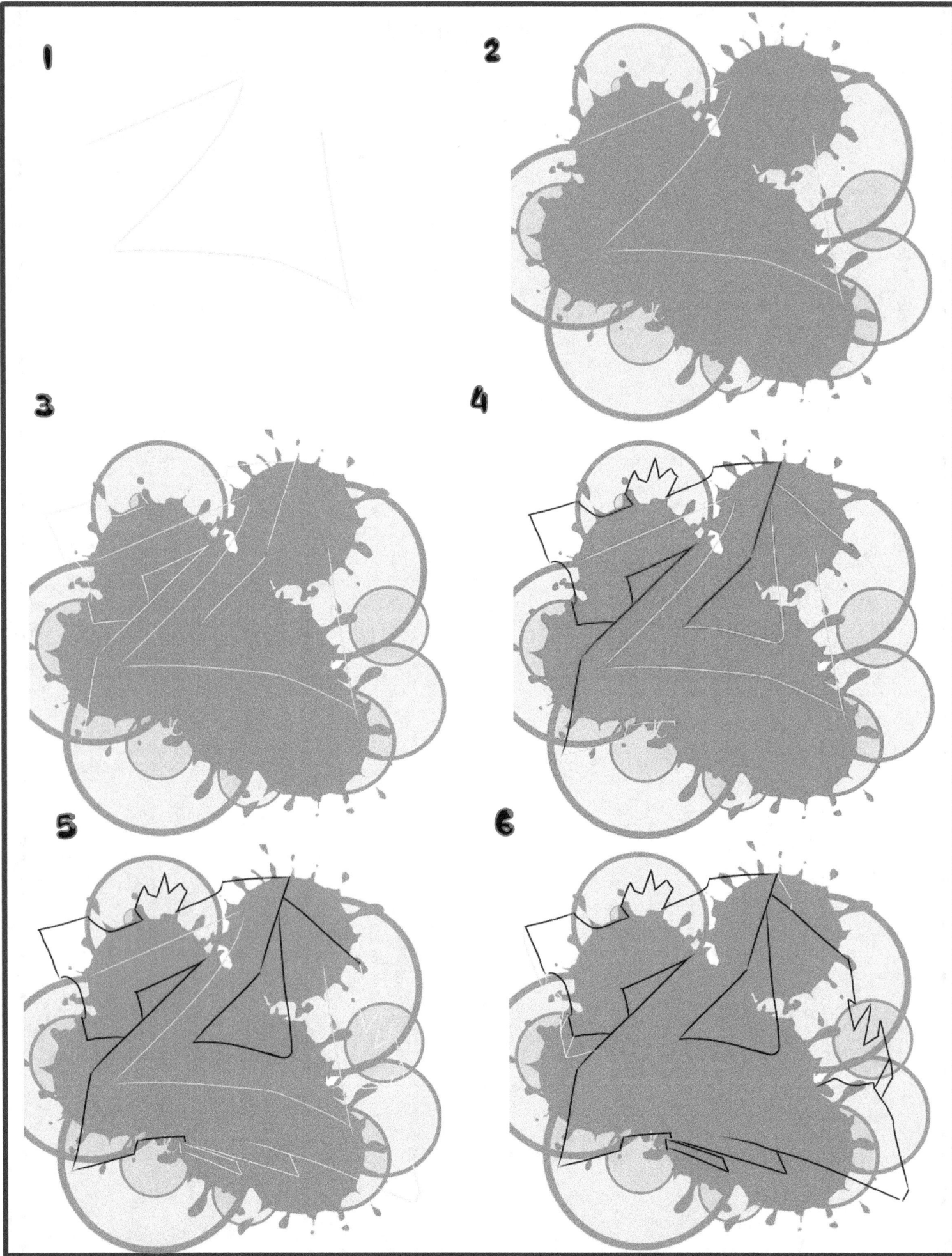

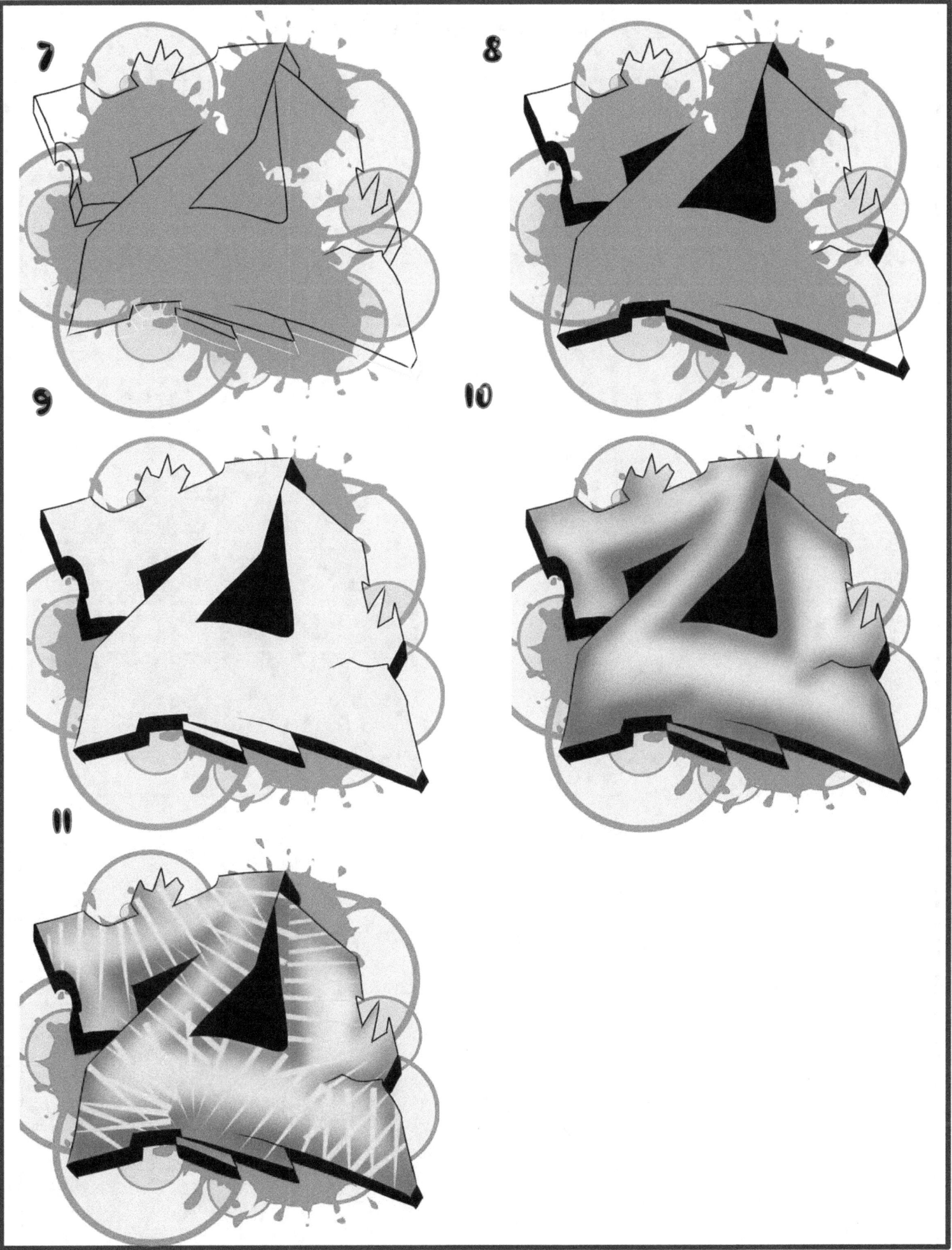

make your own art

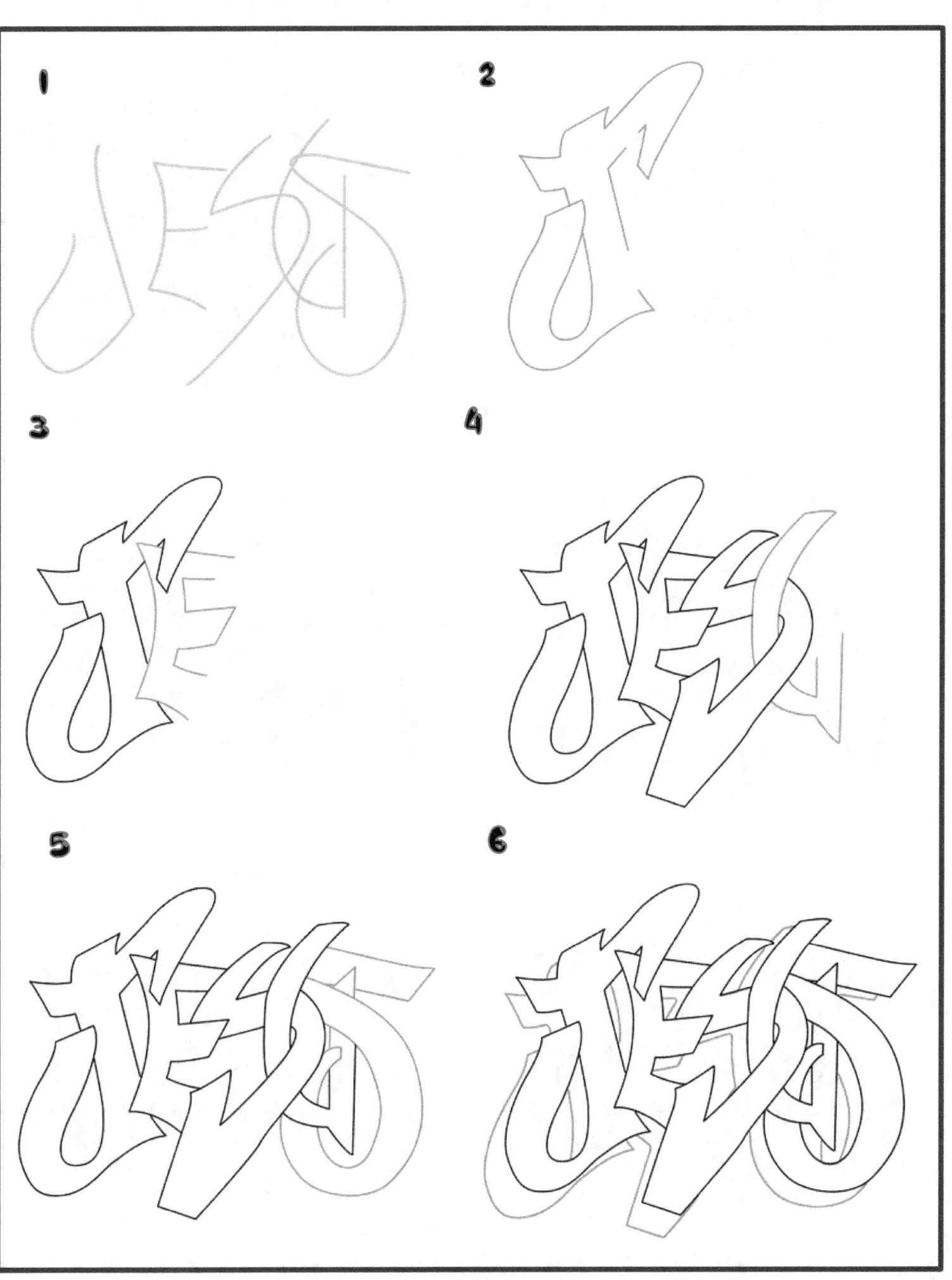

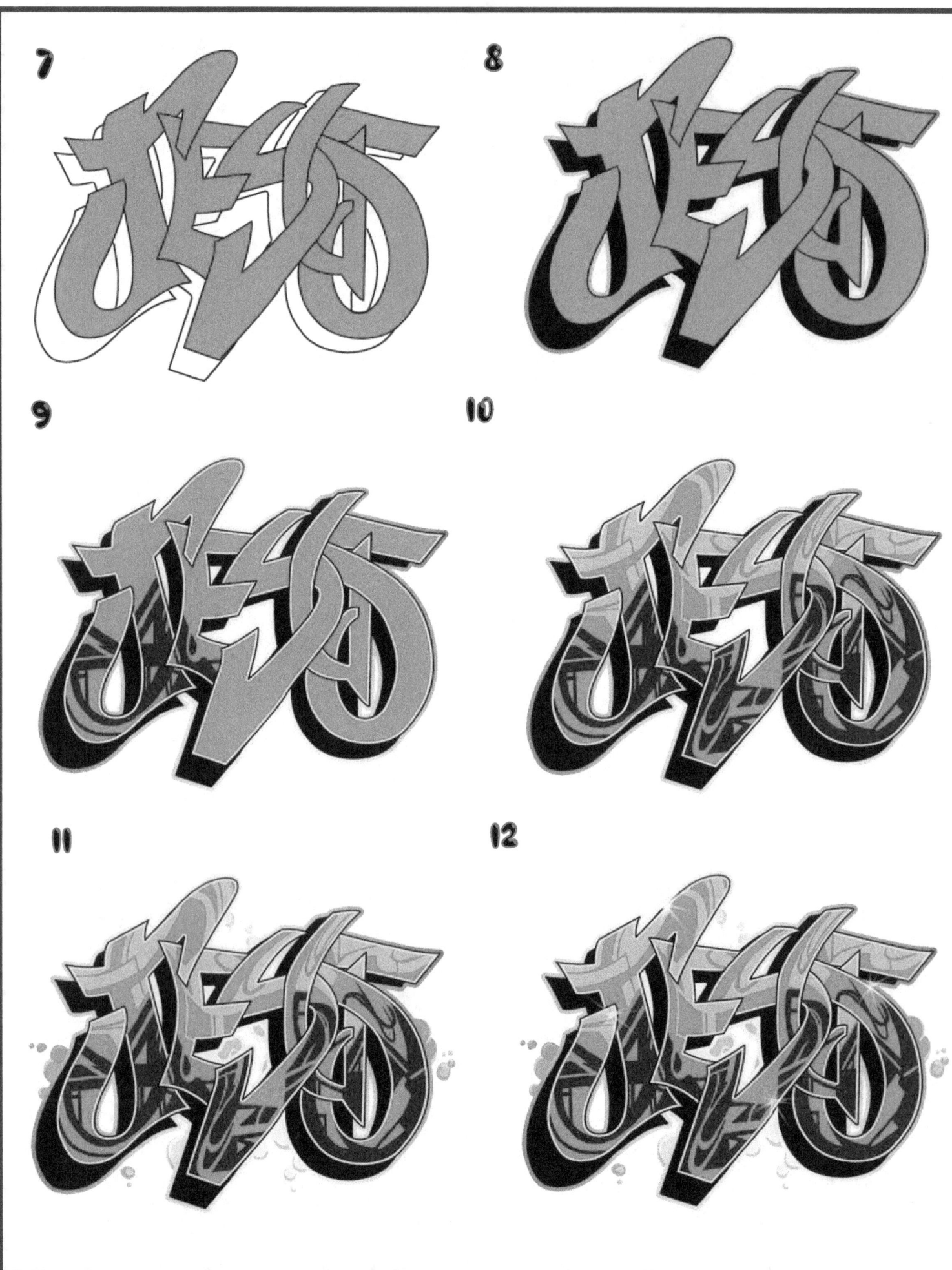

make your own art

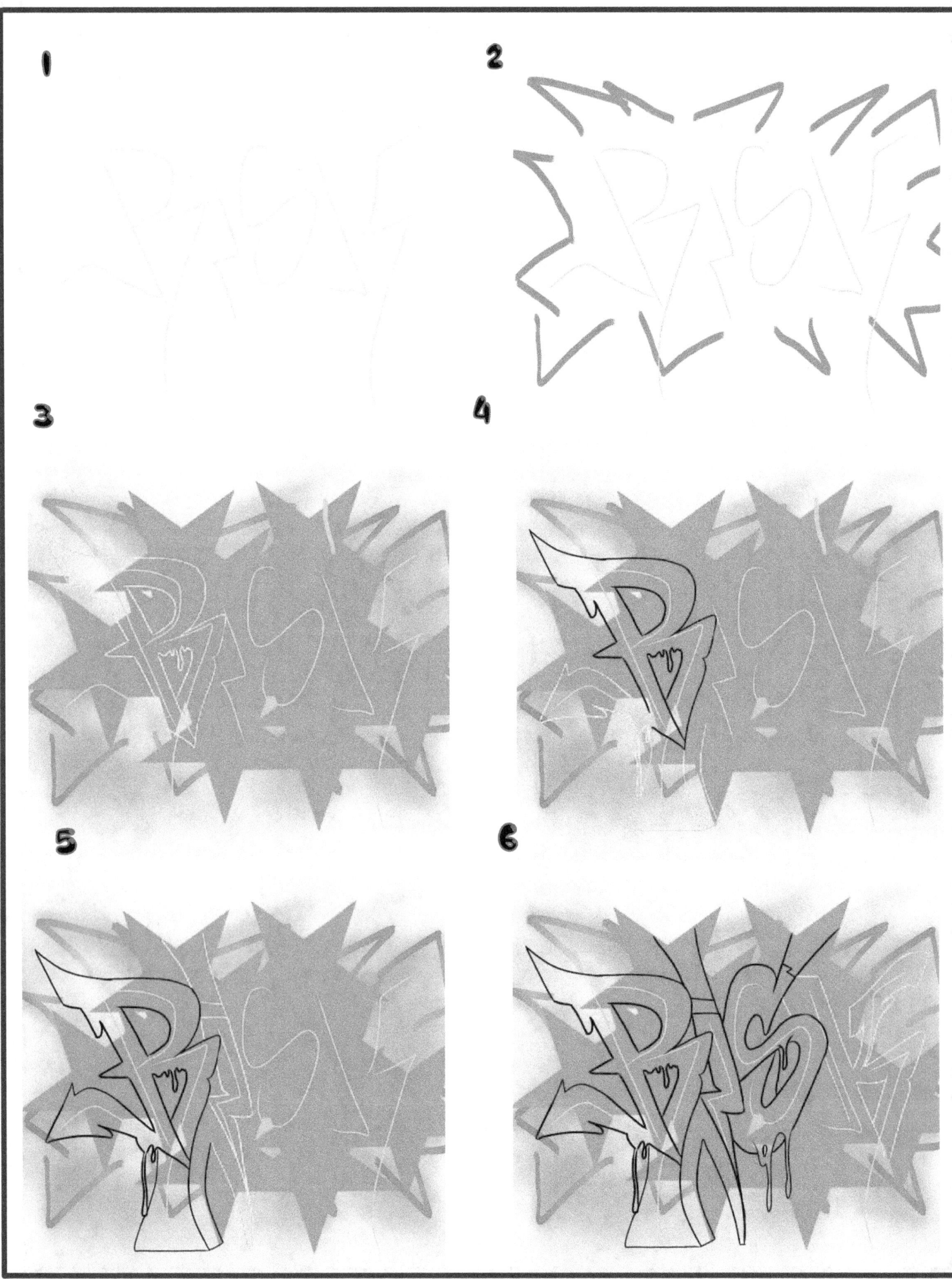

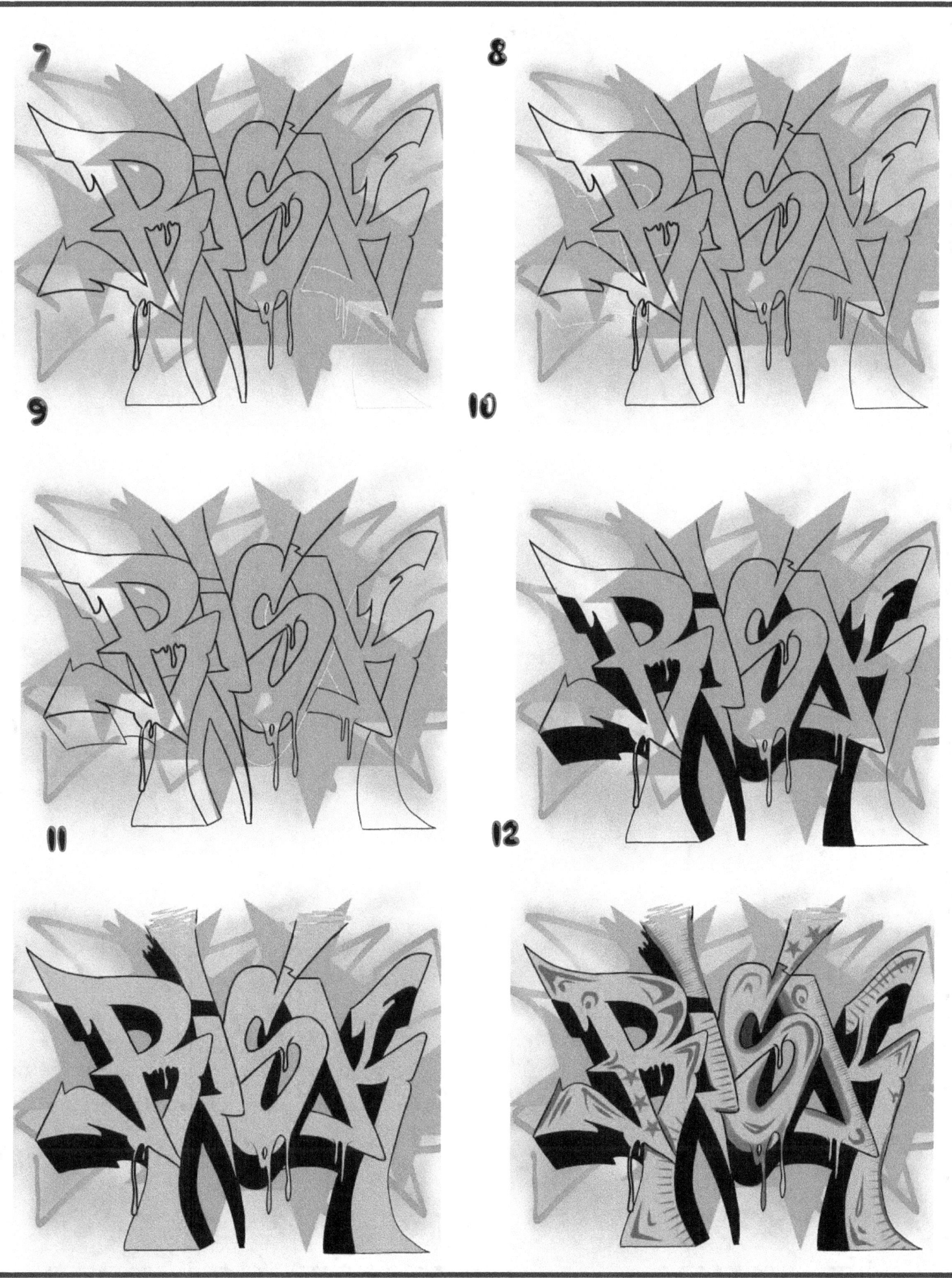

make your own art

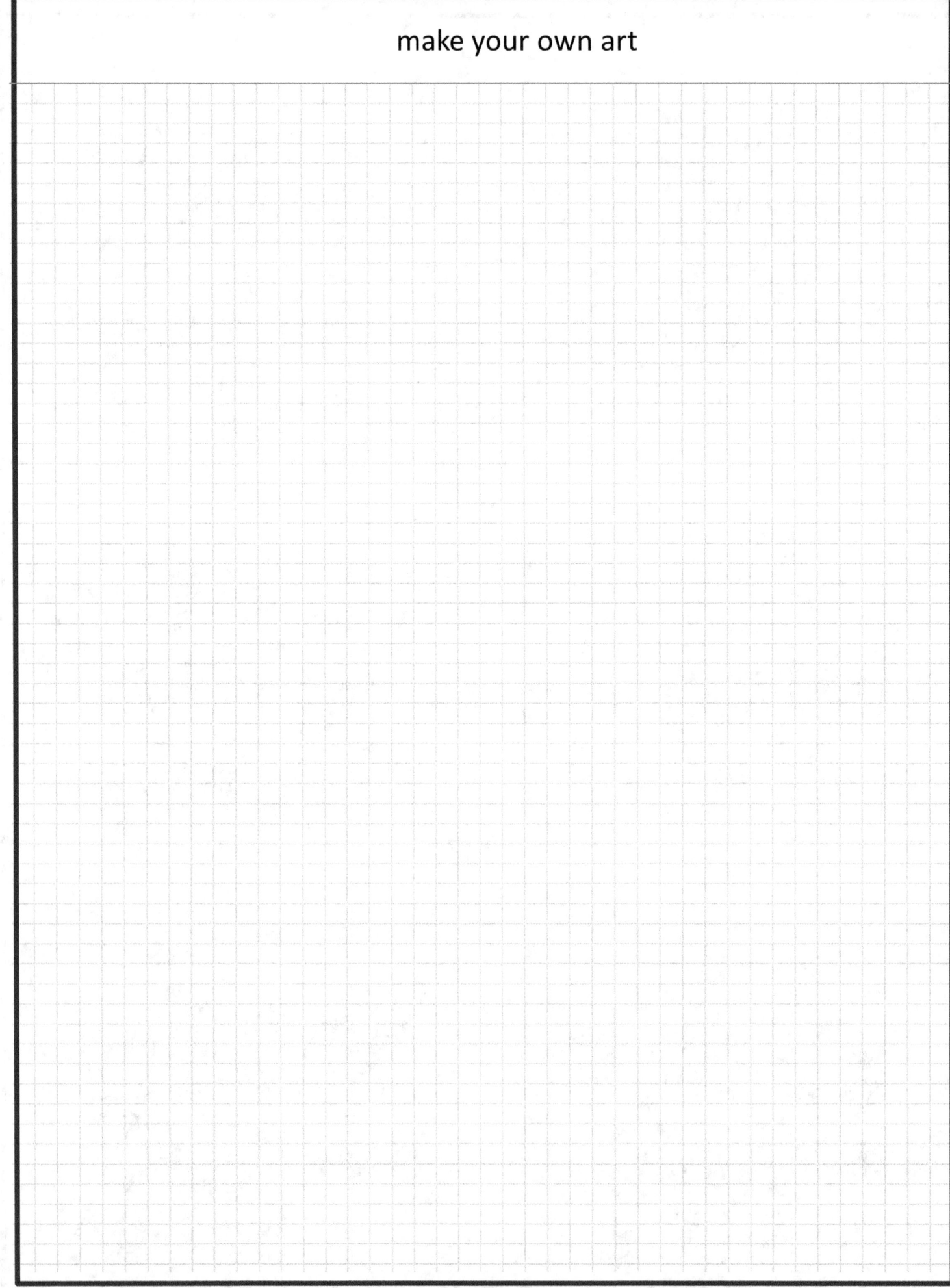

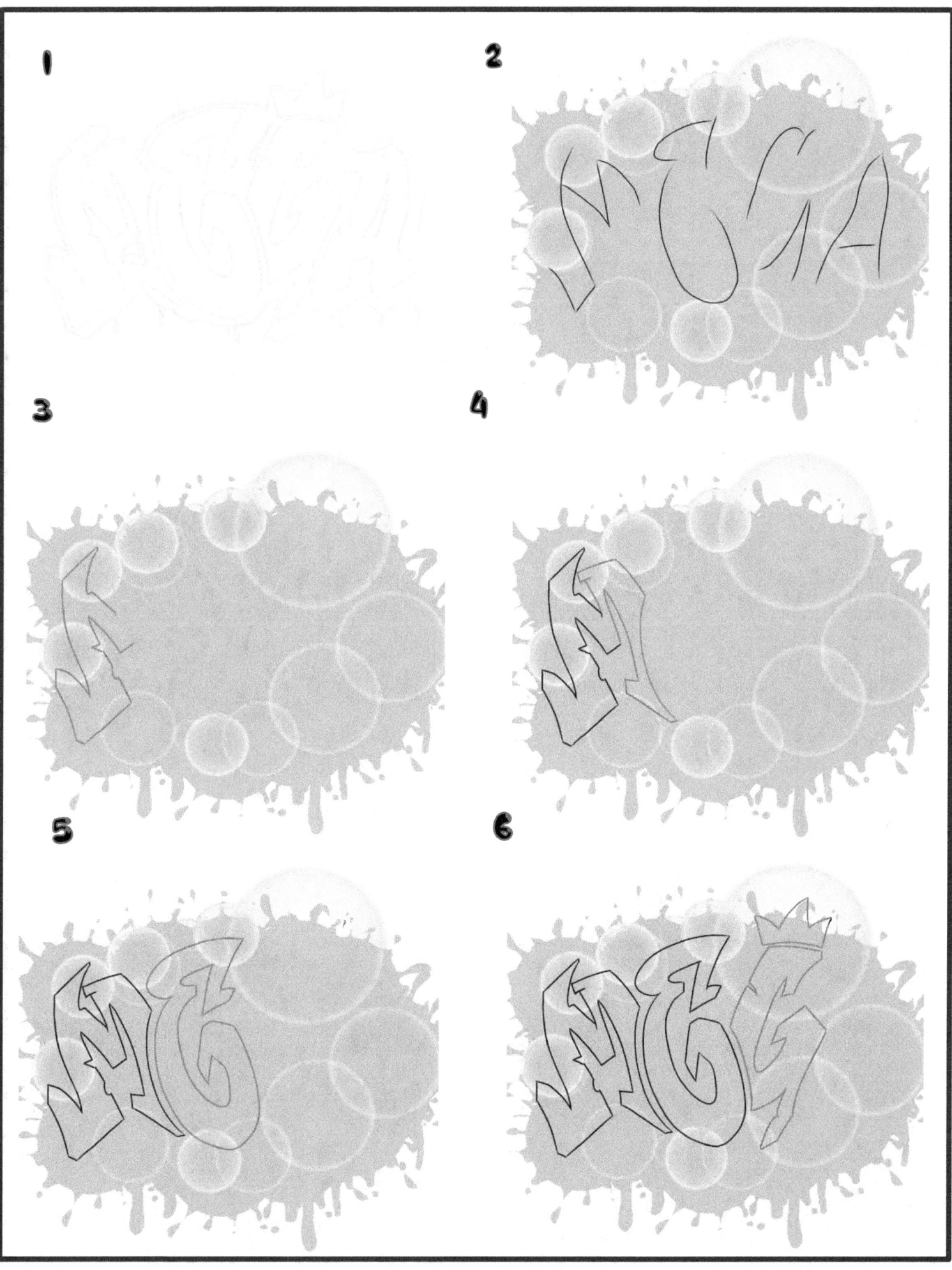

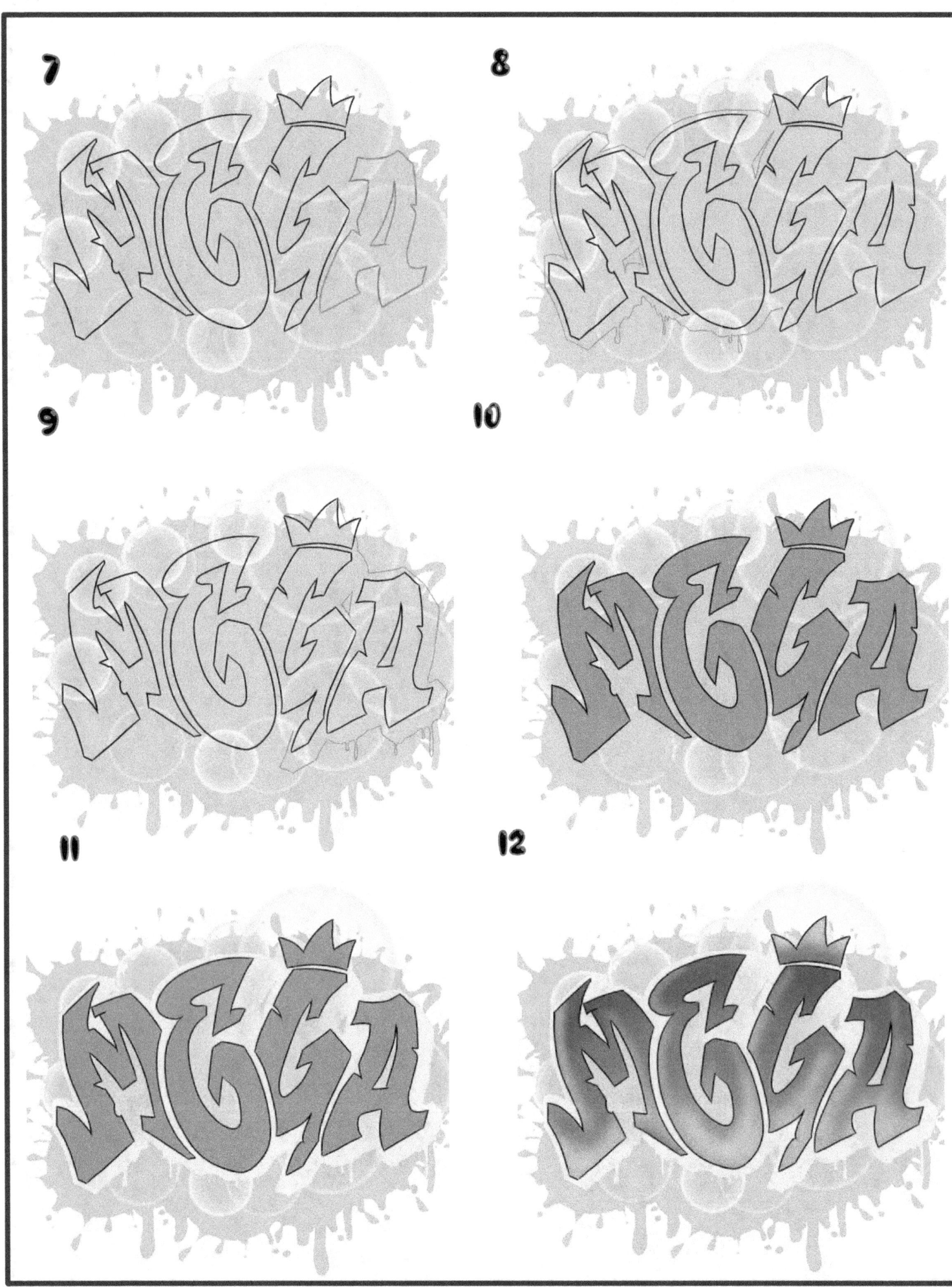

make your own art

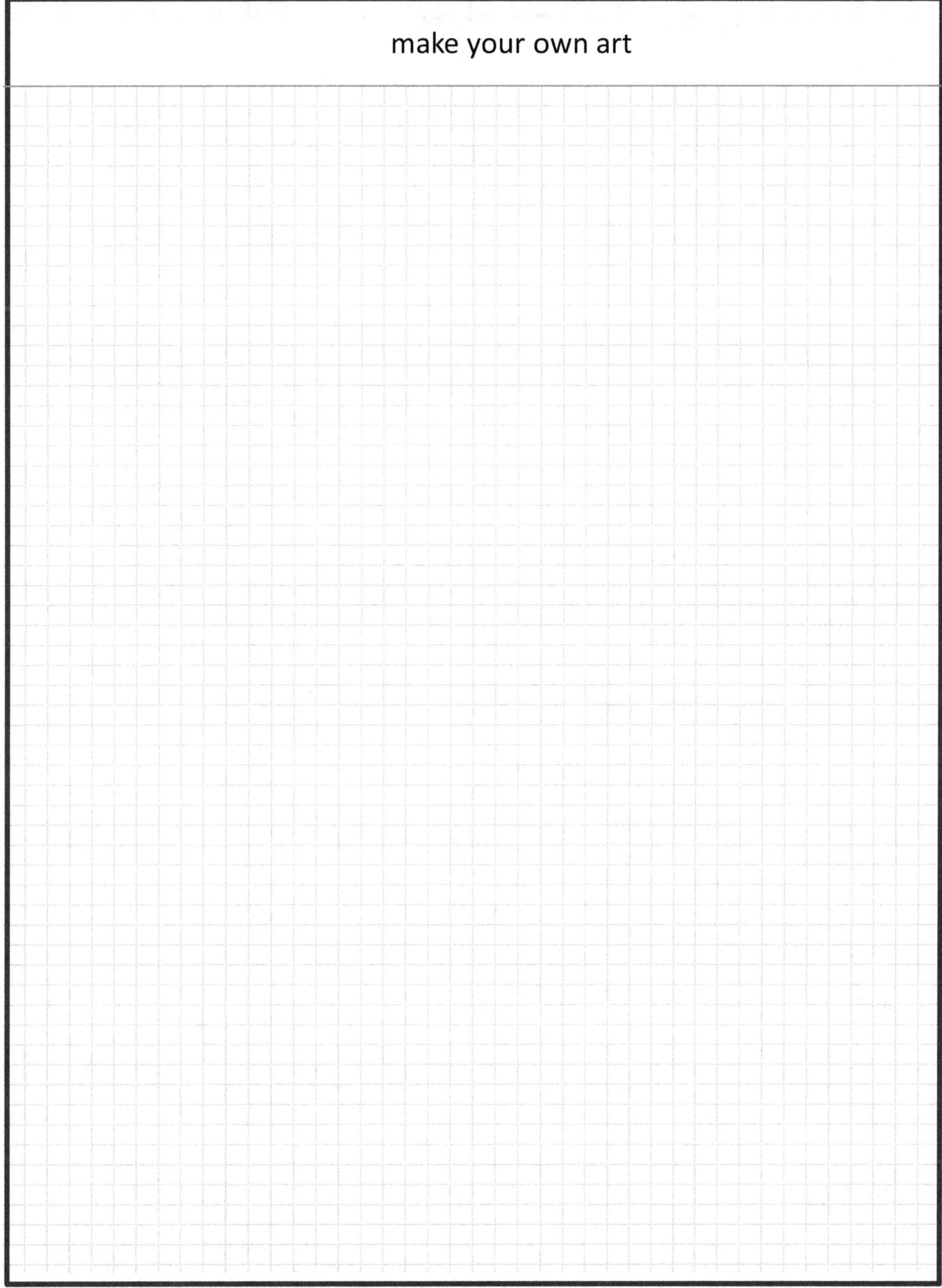

1

2

3

4

5

6

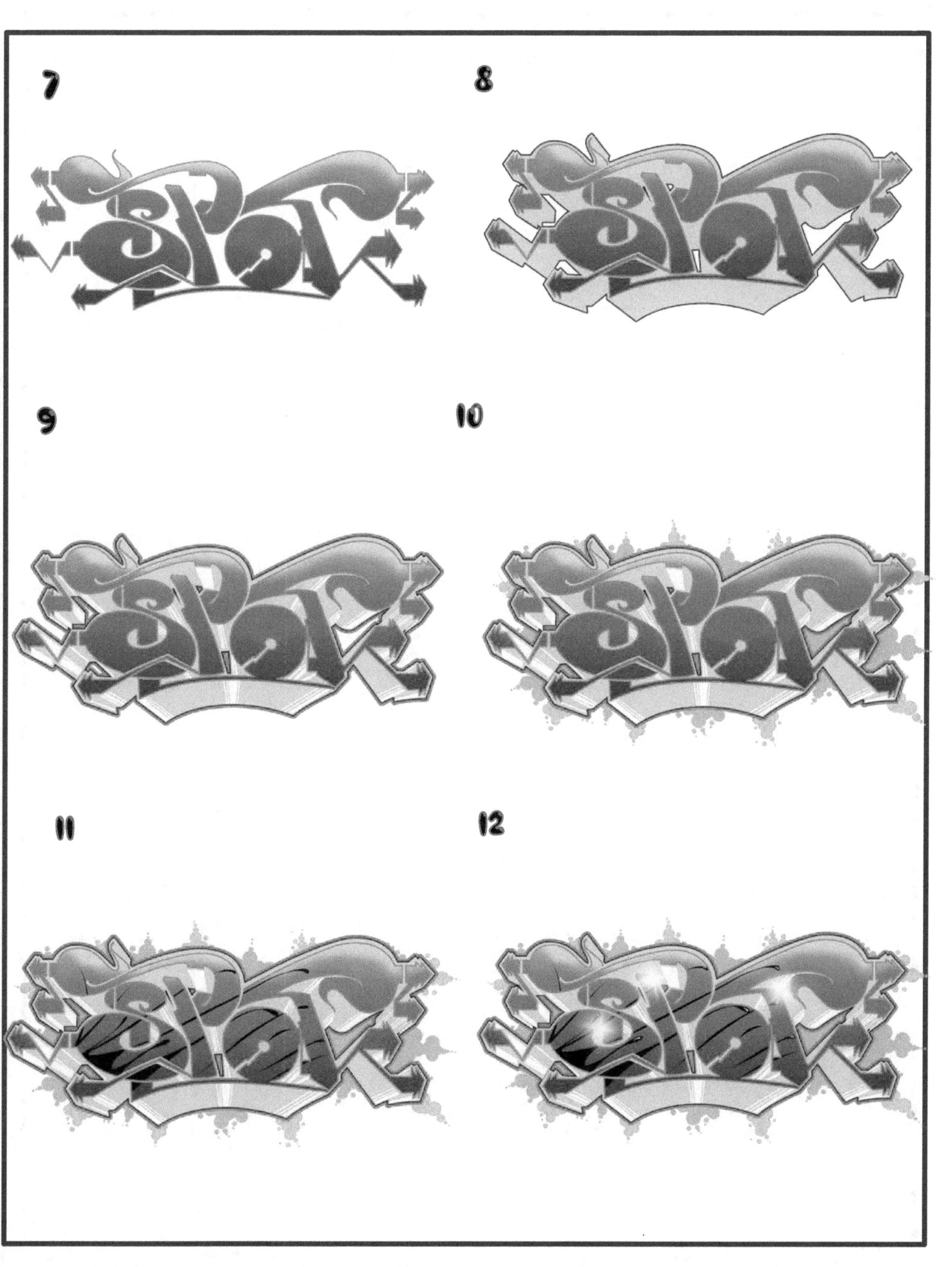

make your own art

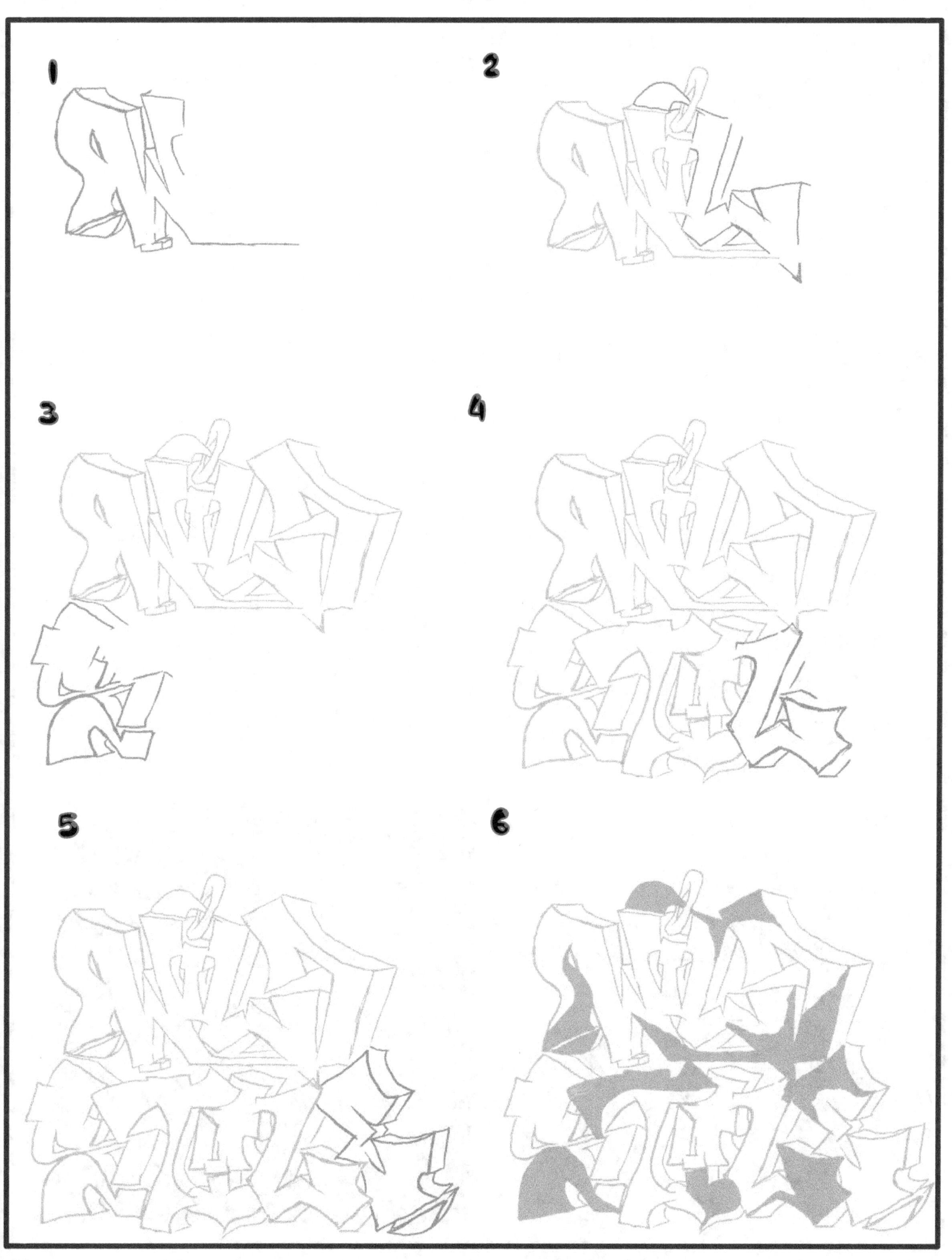

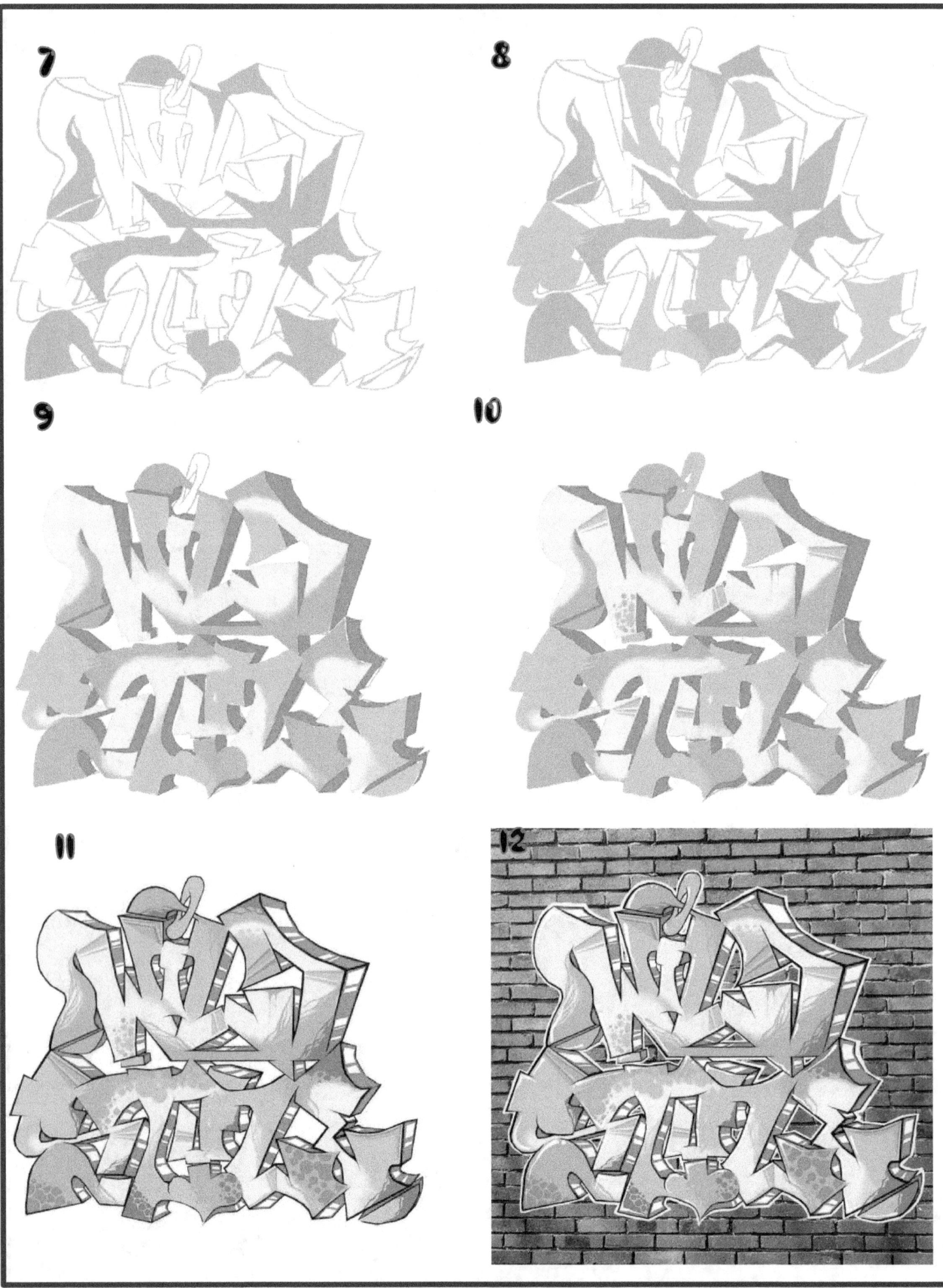

make your own art

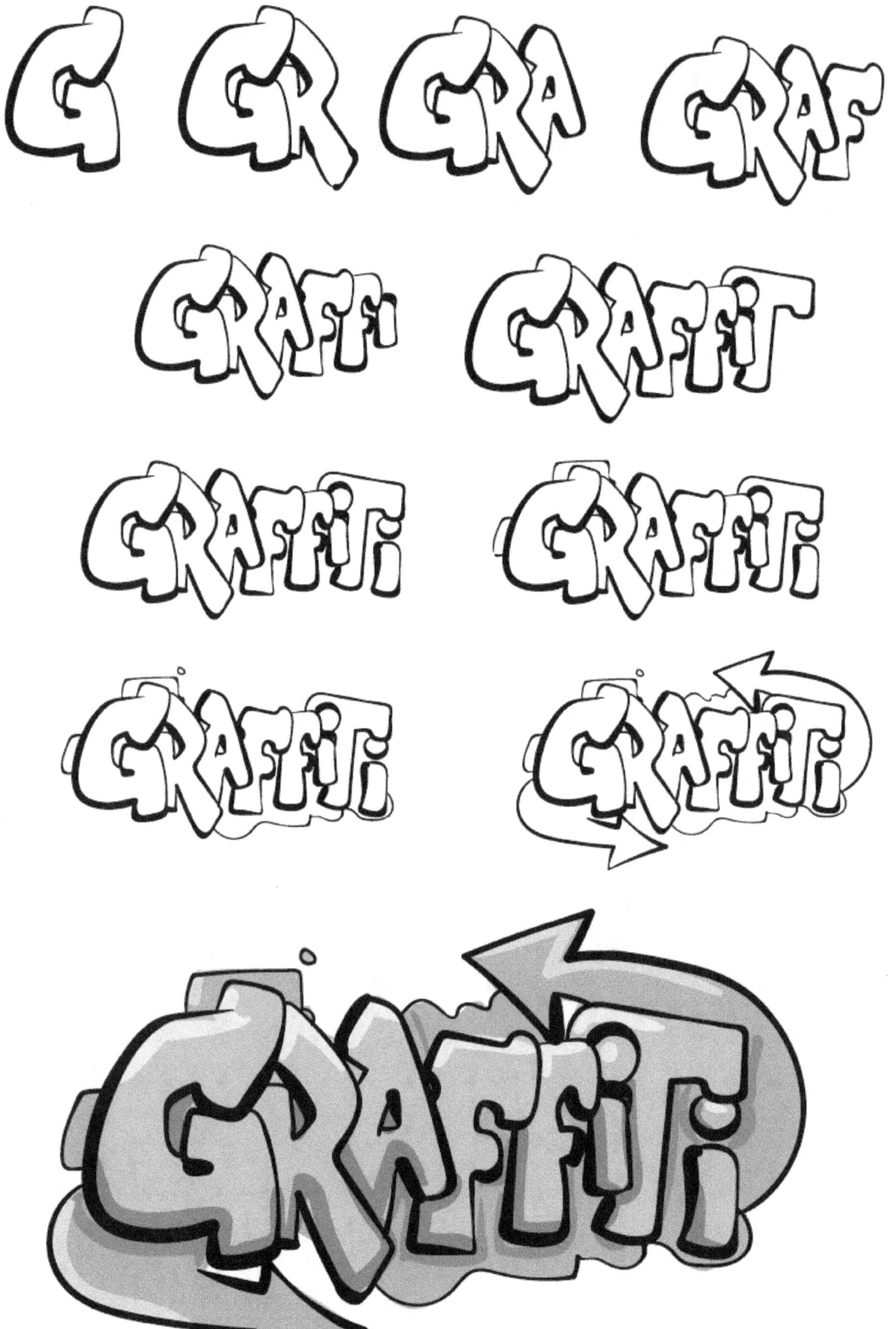
G
GR
GRA
GRAF
GRAFFI
GRAFFIT
GRAFFITI
GRAFFITI
GRAFFITI
GRAFFITI
GRAFFITI

make your own art

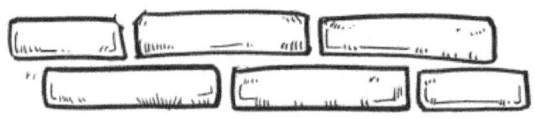

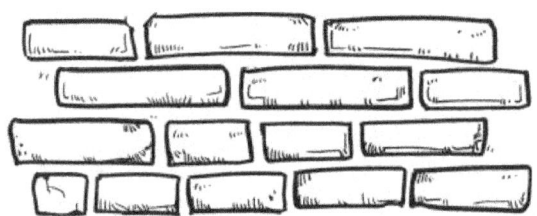

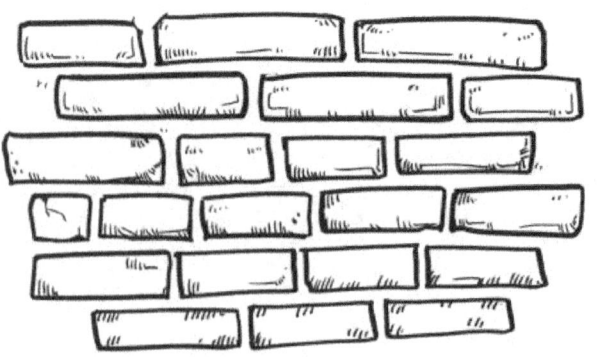

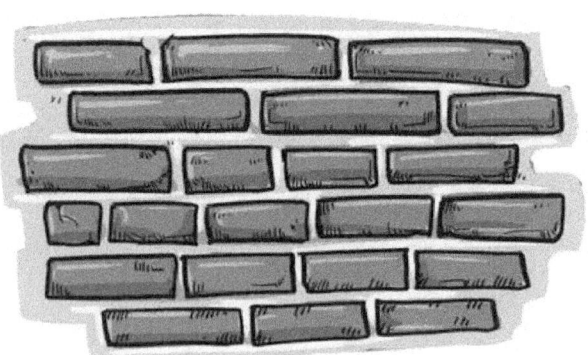

make your own art

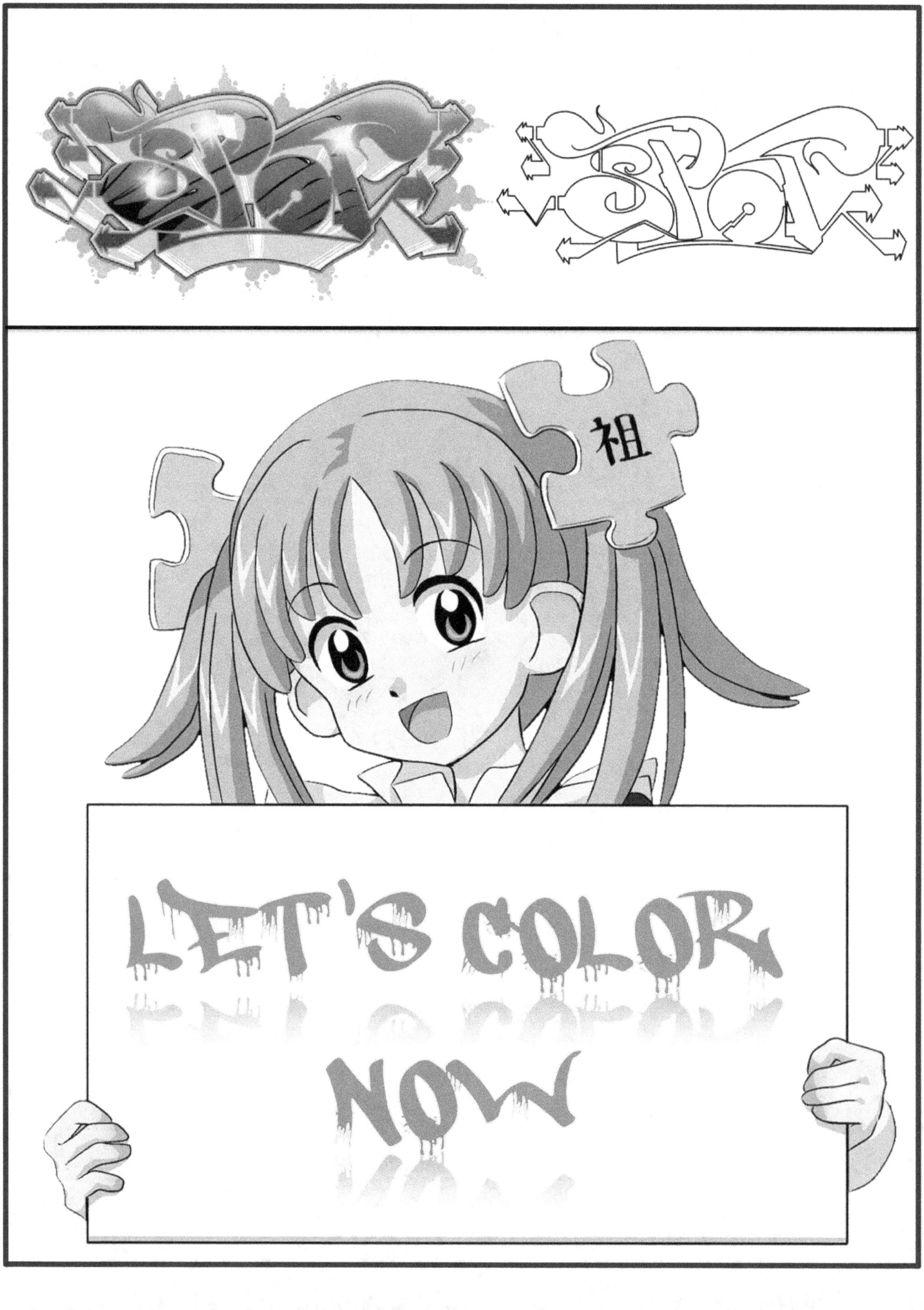

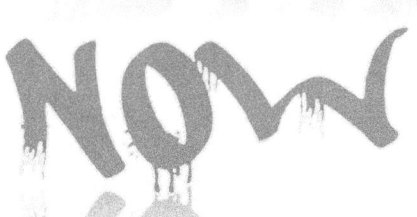

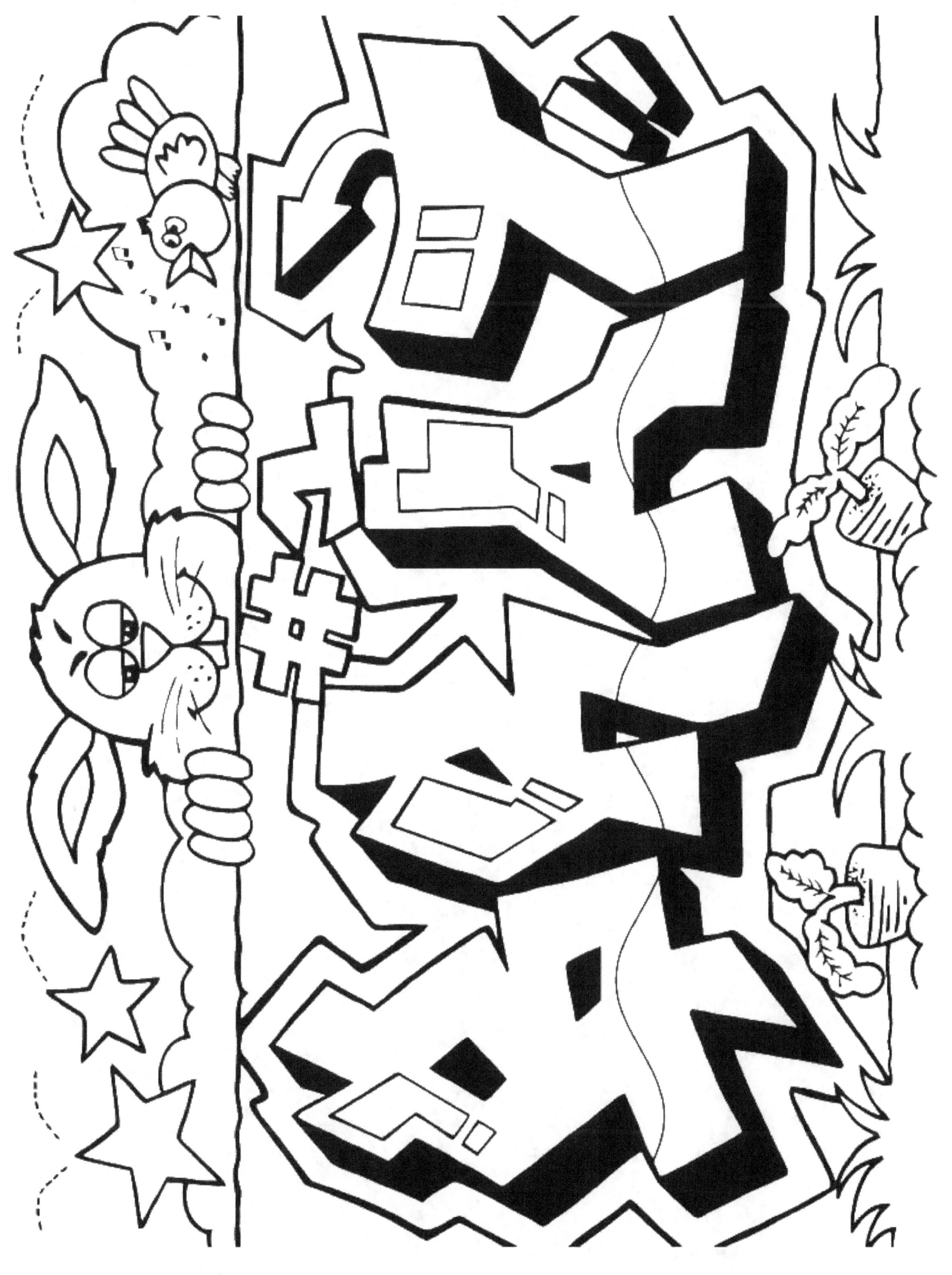

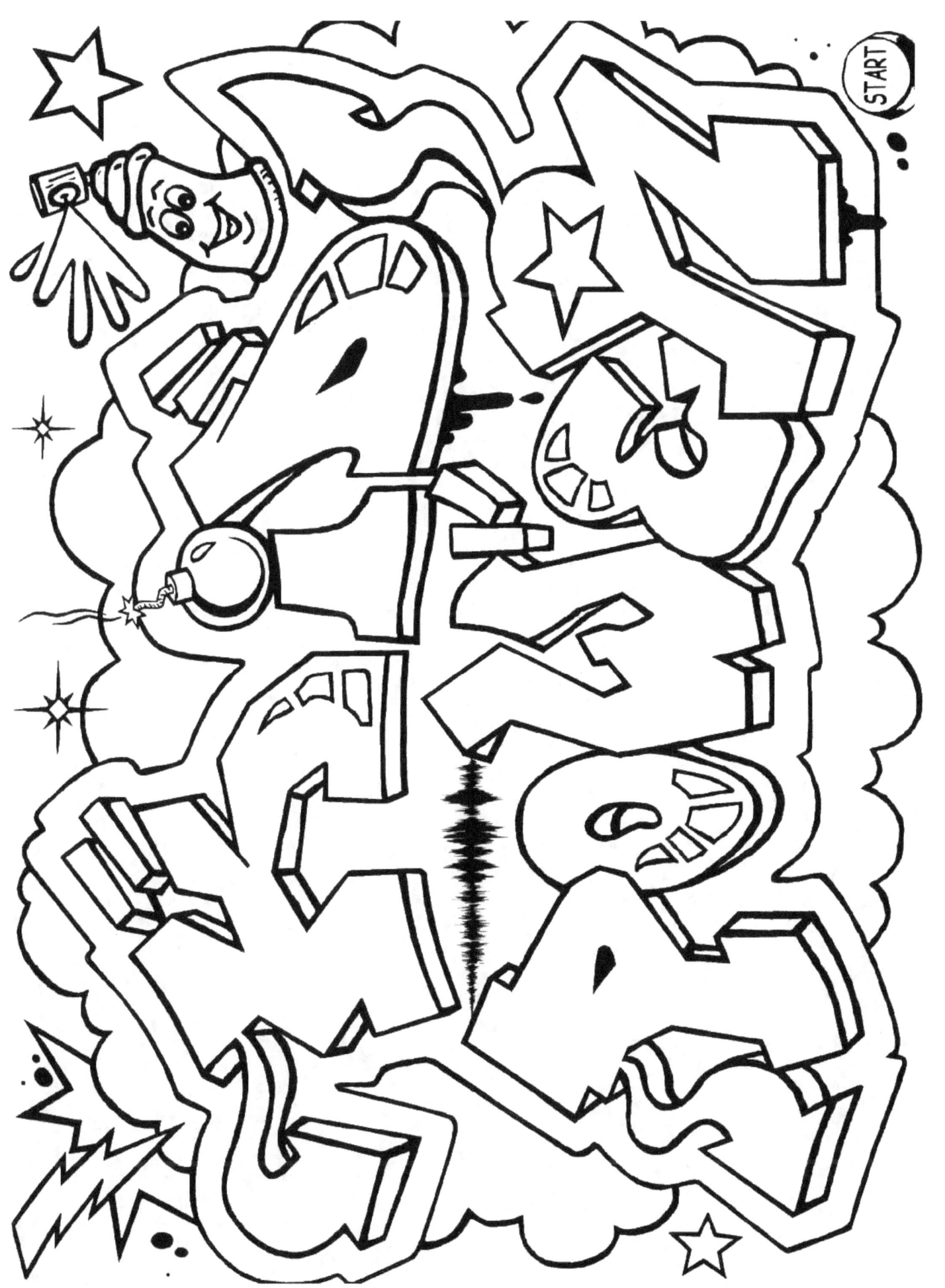

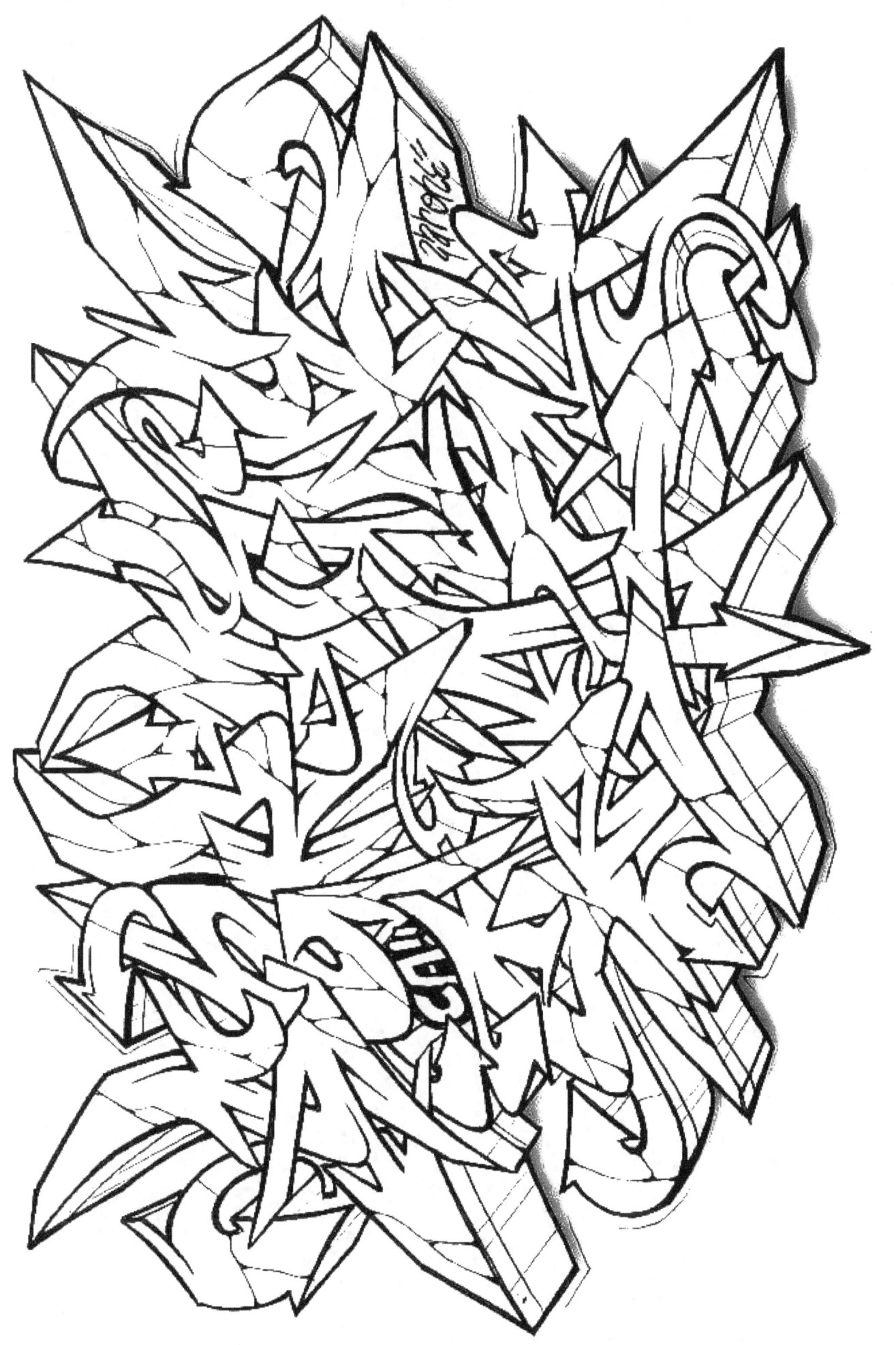

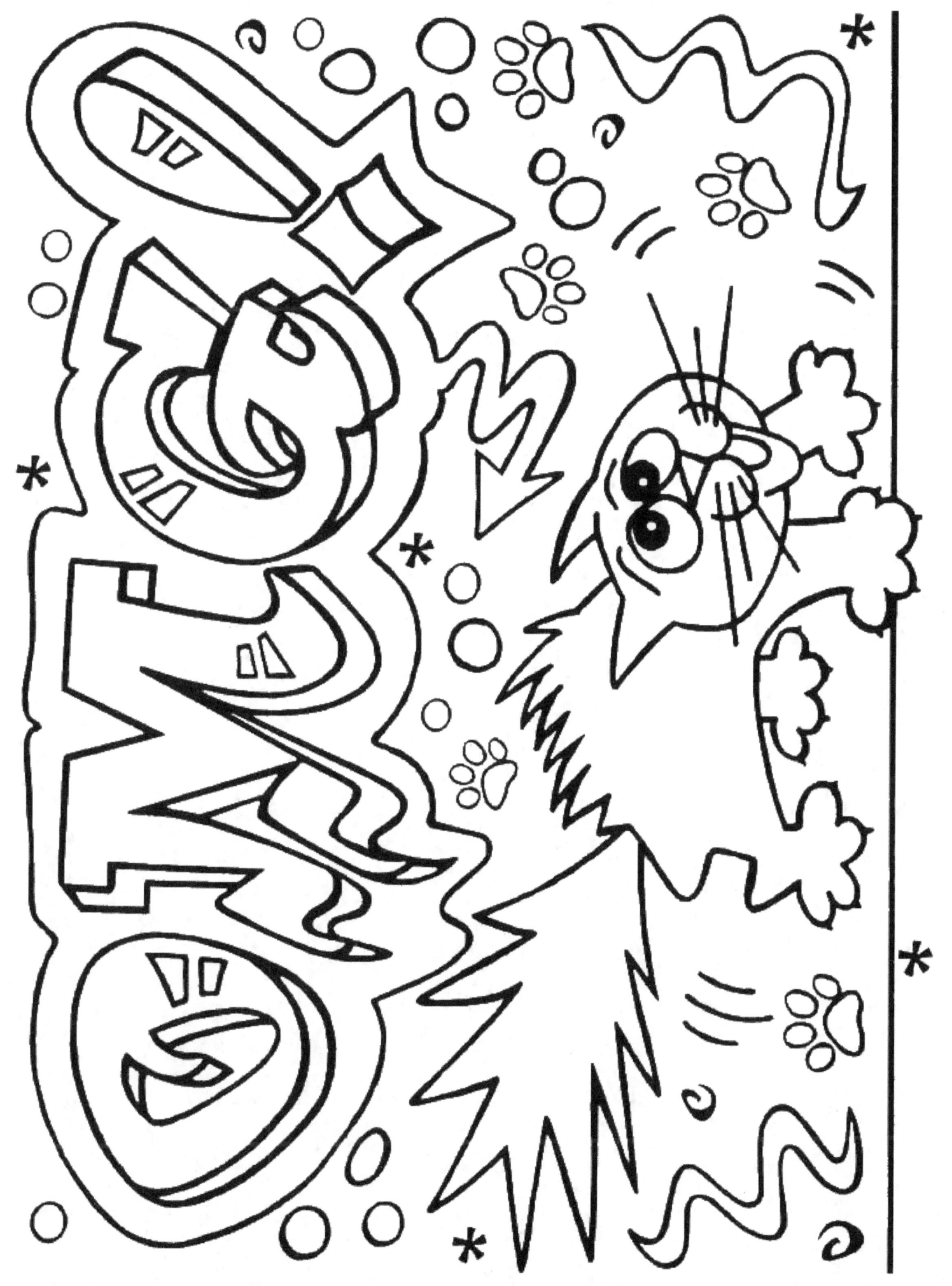

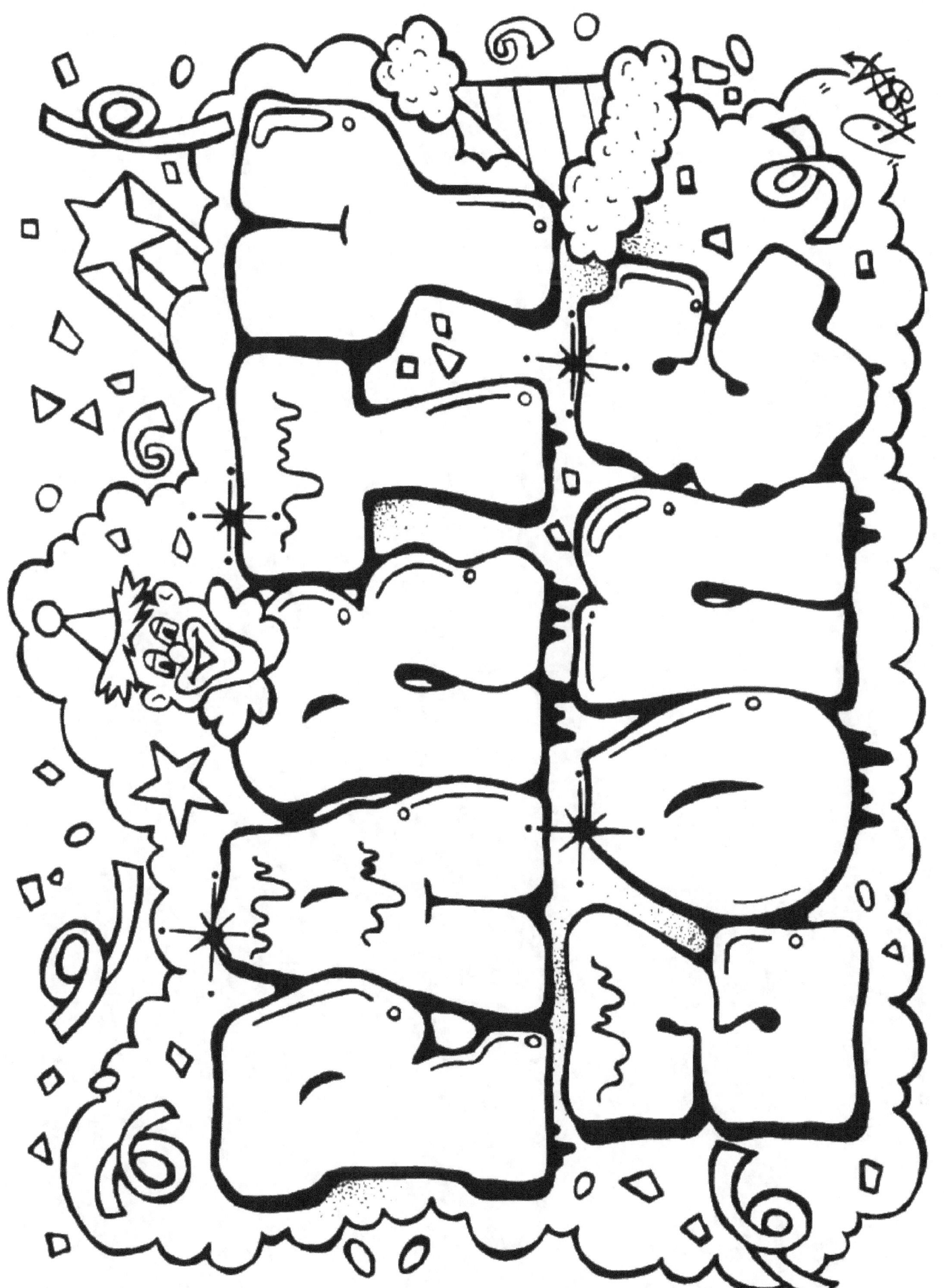

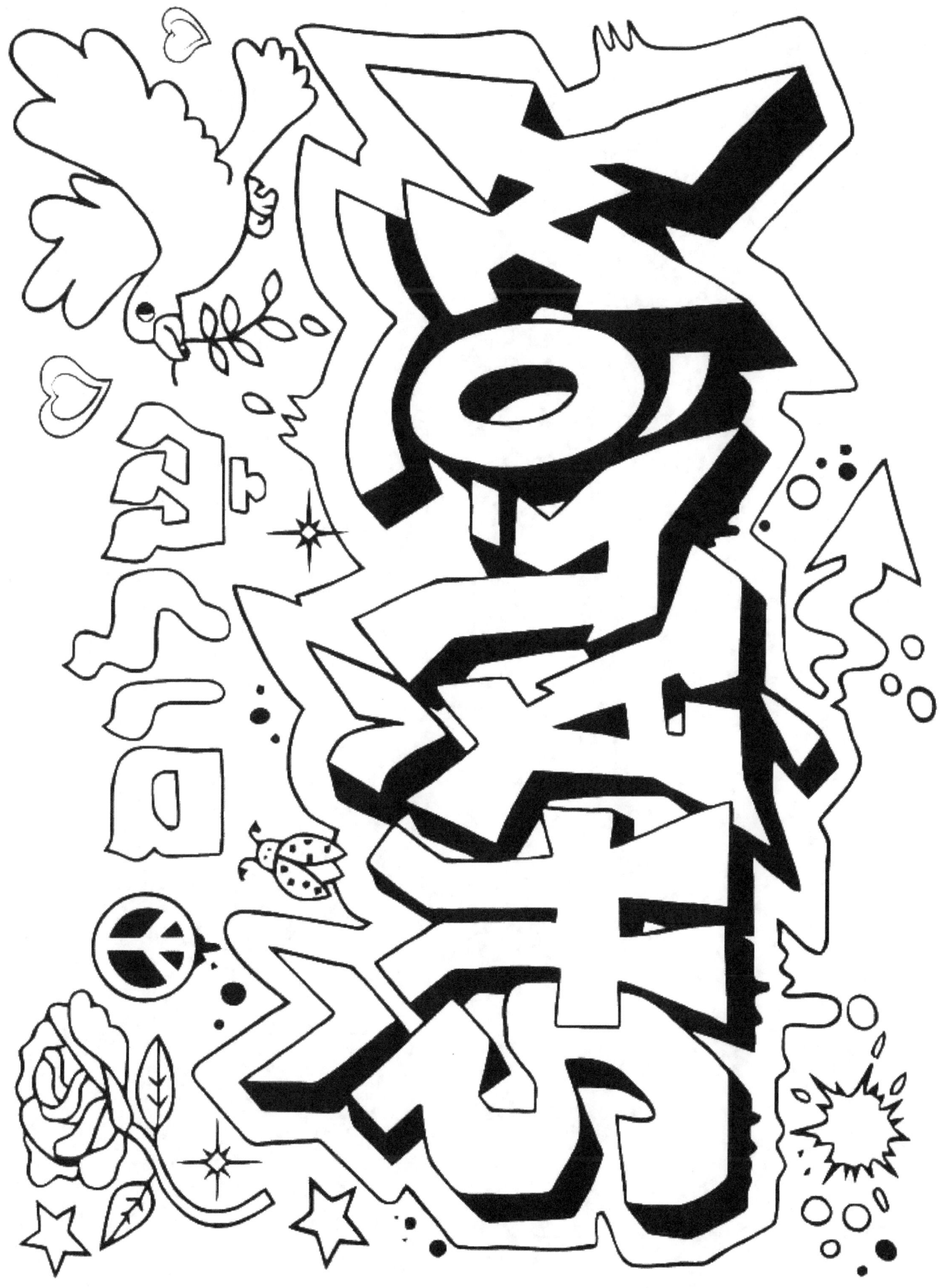

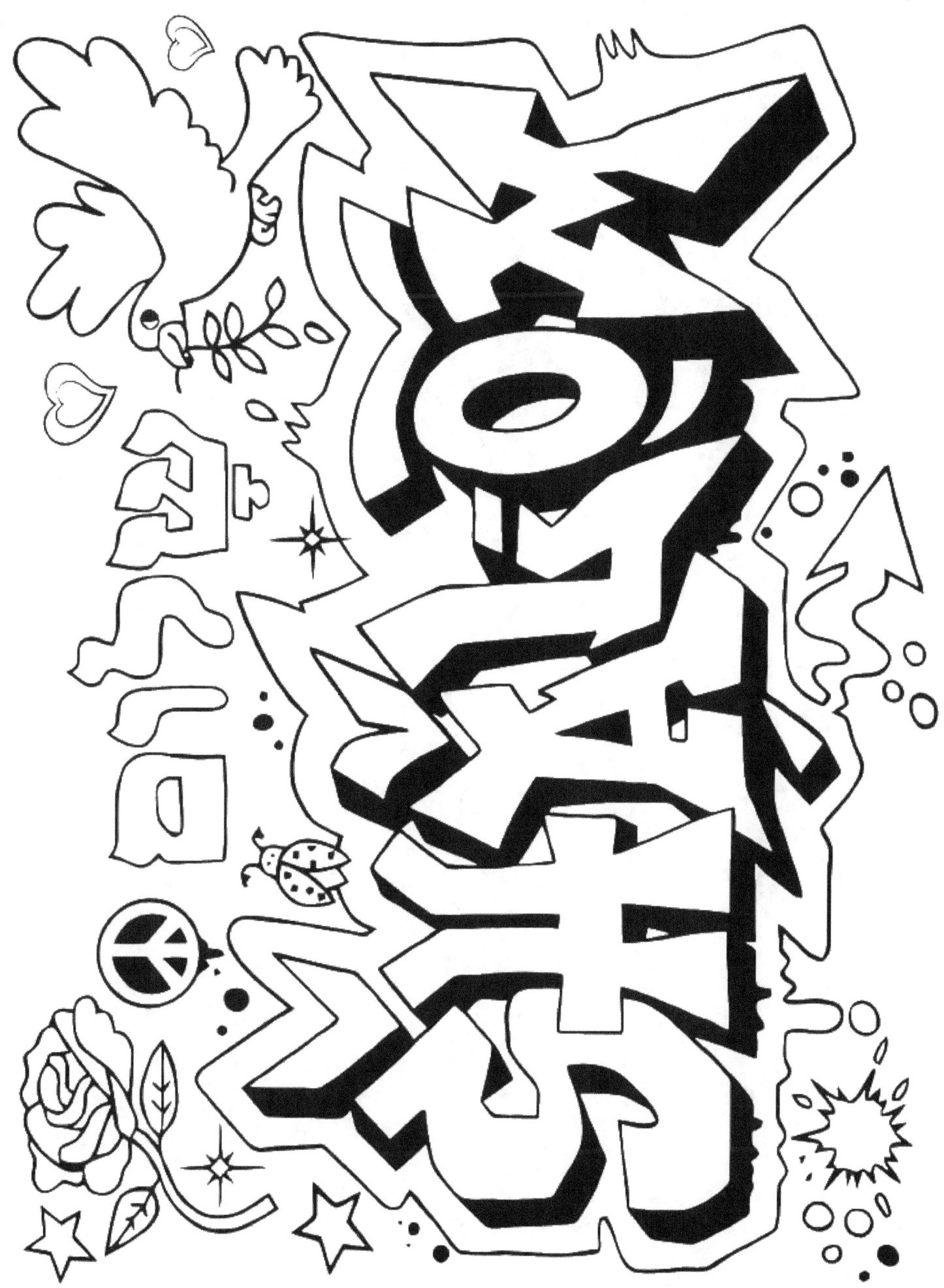

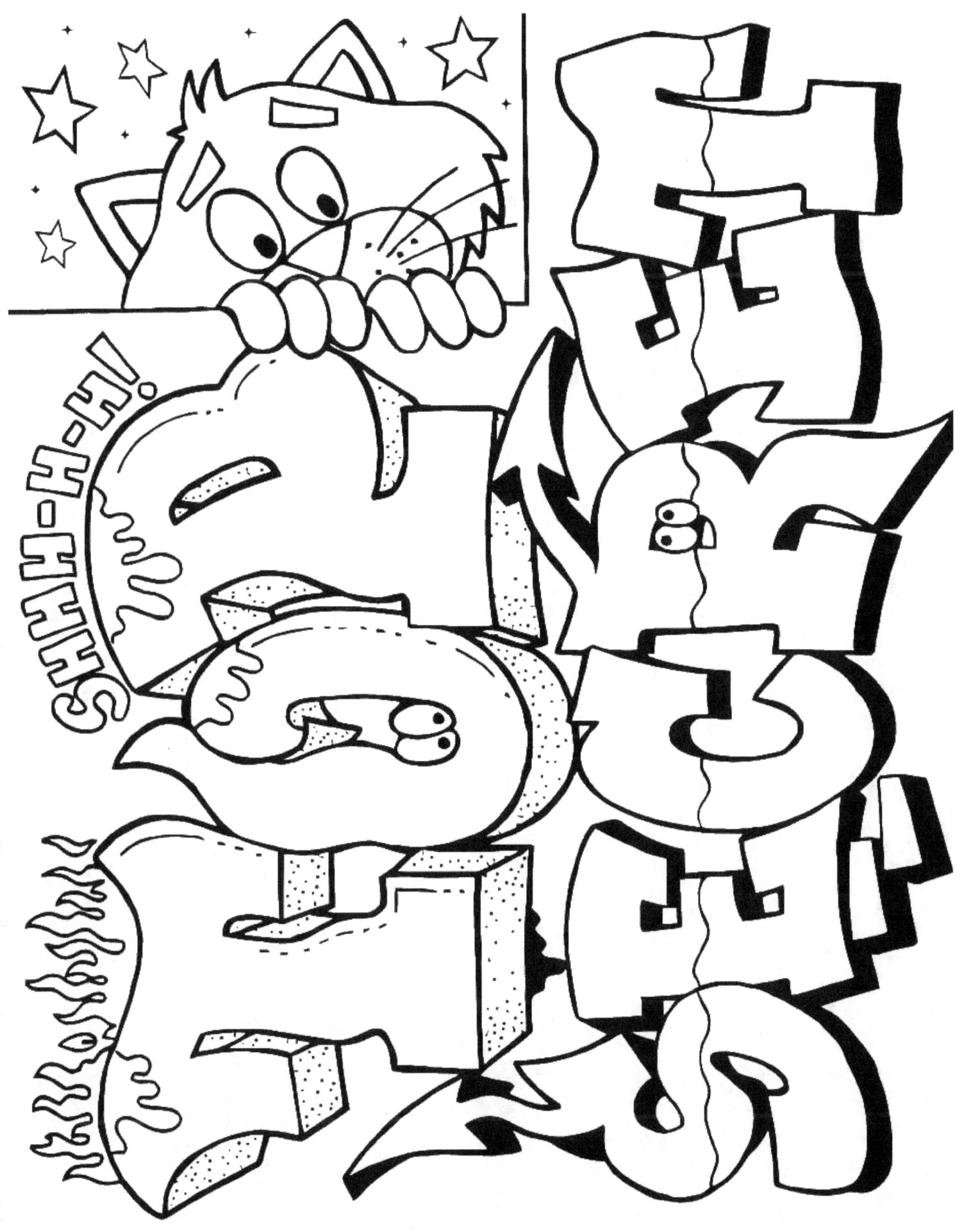

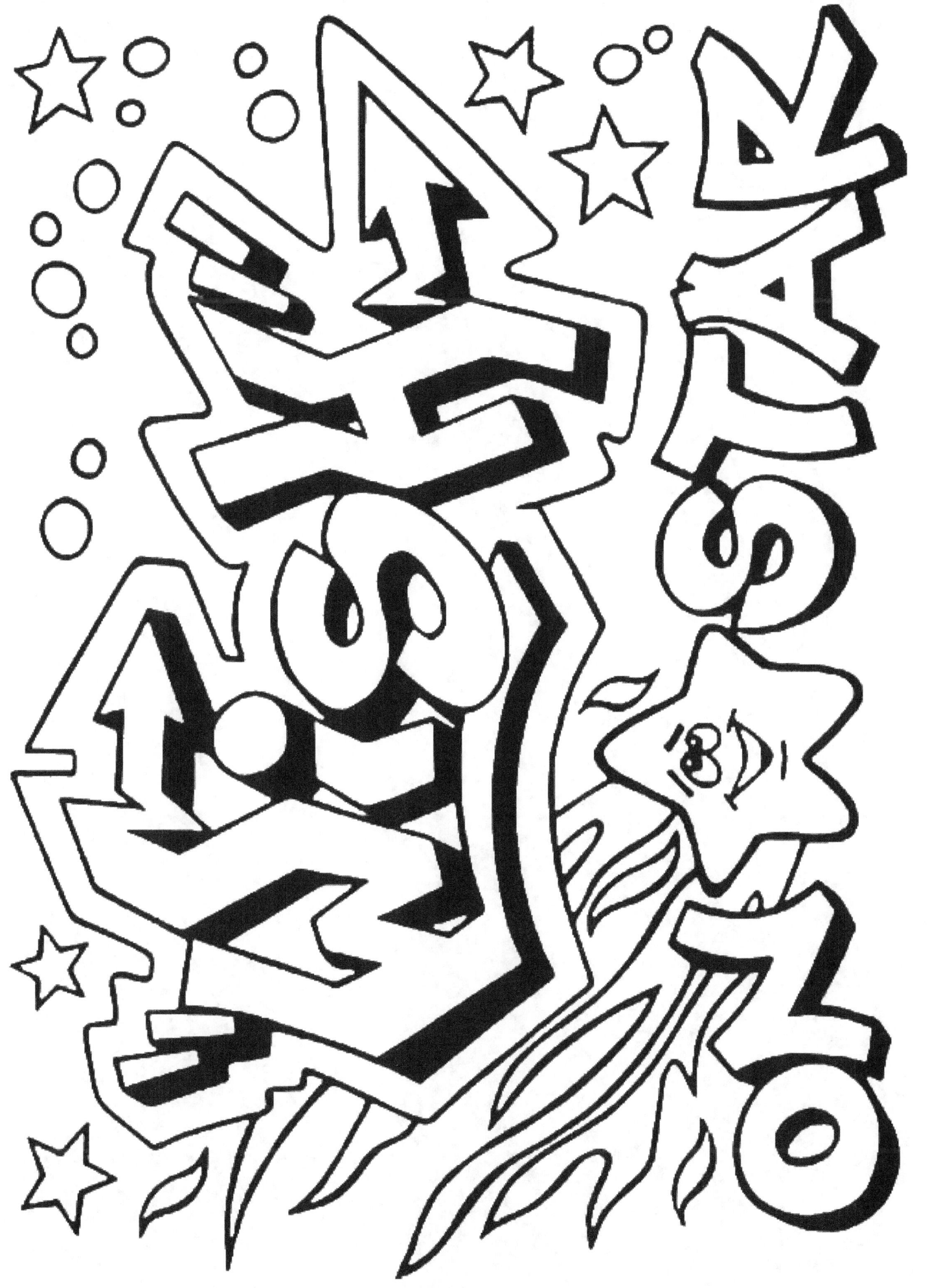

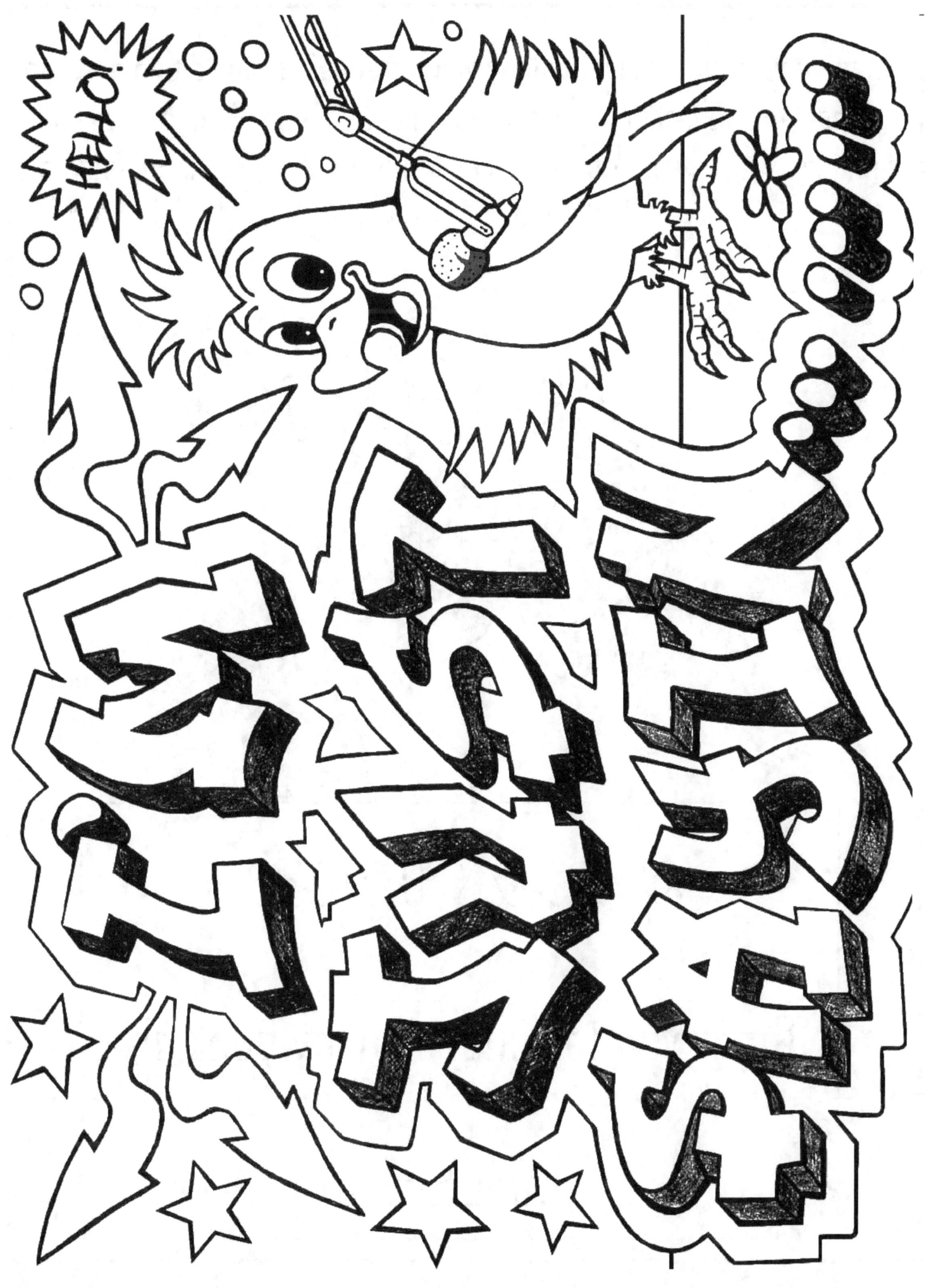

Your support and interest in my work means the world to me. As an author and publisher, my goal is to create engaging and rewarding reading experiences. Your decision to invest in my book validates my efforts and I am truly grateful.

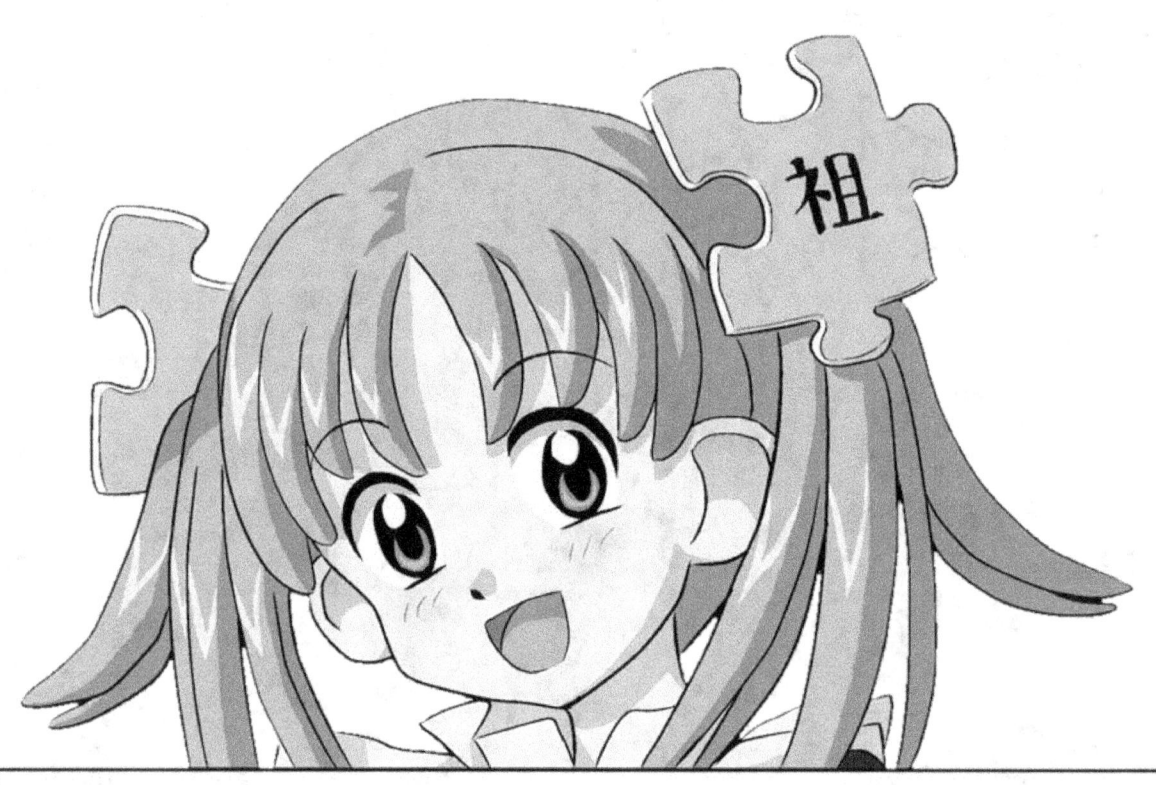

SOPHIA PRESS

Thank you for choosing my book on

Amazon.